Game of My Life

DENVER BRONCOS

Memorable Stories of Broncos Football

JIM SACCOMANO

SPORTS
PUBLISHING

Sports Publishing books may be purchased in bulk at special discounts for sales promotion, corporate gifts, fund-raising, or educational purposes. Special editions can also be created to specifications. For details, contact the Special Sales Department, Sports Publishing, 307 West 36th Street, 11th Floor, New York, NY 10018 or sportspubbooks@skyhorsepublishing.com.

Sports Publishing® is a registered trademark of Skyhorse Publishing, Inc.®, a Delaware corporation.

Visit our website at www.sportspubbooks.com

10 9 8 7 6 5 4 3 2 1

Library of Congress Cataloging-in-Publication Data is available on file.
ISBN: 978-1-61321-070-3

Printed in the United States of America

TO JO ANN

MY CORNERSTONE AND MY MUSE

FOREVER AND EVER...

CONTENTS

Acknowledgments vii

Prologue ix

Chapter 1: Floyd Little 1

Chapter 2: Frank Tripucka 13

Chapter 3: Randy Gradishar 21

Chapter 4: Ed McCaffrey 31

Chapter 5: Goose Gonsoulin 45

Chapter 6: Red Miller 53

Chapter 7: Tom Jackson 63

Chapter 8: Charley Johnson 75

Chapter 9: Rich Karlis 83

Chapter 10: Billy Thompson 93

Chapter 11: Gene Mingo 105

Chapter 12: Haven Moses 115

Chapter 13: Craig Morton 129

Chapter 14: Jack Dolbin 141

Chapter 15: Steve Atwater 155

Chapter 16: Jim Turner 167

Chapter 17: Karl Mecklenburg 179

Chapter 18: Shannon Sharpe 191

Chapter 19: Terrell Davis 205

Chapter 20: John Elway 219

Chapter 21: Rod Smith 233

ACKNOWLEDGMENTS

The author wishes to thank a number of individuals for their assistance.

Special thanks go out to the 20 former Denver Broncos players and coaches who graciously gave of their time and cooperation in the interview process.

Thanks as well to Dave Gaylinn, Rebecca Villanueva, Kate Doll, and Denver Parler for their assistance in the research and transcription process.

Also, thanks to the Denver Broncos and Clarkson and Associates for the photographs used in this book.

PROLOGUE

In my 30 seasons working for the city's first major-league sports franchise, I have grown to strongly hold the opinion that the Denver Broncos are the soul of the city, and that belief has only been reinforced in getting the opportunity to write this book.

Not only has the city expressed unbridled love and passion for the Broncos over the past five decades, but in talking to the 20 notables who make up this book, it was apparent how much that feeling was mutually held by the players.

The attachment of Denver's fans to their football team stands out as unusual, but there were numerous times during the interview process when the subject would have to stop and compose himself. Invariably, that would happen when discussing the fans, and that tremendous bond between fan and player.

Since the team began serving as the lightning rod for national attention in Denver, the passion has always seemed greater here than in many other cities.

But we always think of that emotional attachment as belonging to the fans, not taking into account that to the players it is a two-way street.

I didn't quite know what to expect as I began the process of talking to players about that game that meant the most to them, but ultimately I was humbled by the process.

At all levels, it was deeper, richer, more gratifying, and more satisfying than I anticipated going in. Their stories touched me, and I hope they touch the reader as well.

Each player told his own unique story, and together they weaved a tapestry of pro football and Bronco history in Denver, from the humblest beginnings to a present that has the team firmly established as one of the most successful franchises in America's most popular sport.

I found that each player had his own driving force, his own reason to pick that particular game. Time after time it came back to people—the fans or the parents—being the common ground.

They were good enough to give me their time and their memories, and I found myself trying to do the right thing by every story, some now several decades old, because if the player was willing to give his time to the telling of it, I needed to do justice to the ultimate reading of it.

Some of those stories involve championships, and others seem ordinary save for extraordinary personal meaning. In each case, it was the player who singled out the game—that moment in time, which to him is the most defining of his professional football career.

I hope justice has been done to their memories in this book, that the fan feels the passion and emotion of each player coming through the pages, and that together we can all light a candle to the state religion one more time.

—Jim Saccomano

Chapter 1

FLOYD LITTLE

BEFORE THE BRONCOS

Floyd Little symbolized pro football in Denver for many years, certainly for the entire period before the Broncos made the playoffs and became annual championship contenders.

So meager was the state of the Denver franchise over most of its first two decades that Little was given and has since carried the nickname, "The Franchise."

It seems only fitting that a book about the team start with The Franchise.

A Hall-of-Fame-quality player and then a successful businessman, Little's beginnings were humble. "Very, very difficult and very challenging," he recalls. "There was a lot of adversity, and I was able to deal with those adversities on a daily basis to get better. I think the situation that really stands out with me was one when I was young. Growing up my mom had six kids—I lost my dad when I was five or six years old—and I remember one day coming home from school and they had evicted us from our apartment. Our furniture was out on the sidewalk and the kids from the neighborhood were jumping up and down on the furniture and my mom was sitting on the couch crying. I remember putting my arms around her and telling her that as long as I lived they would never do that again to her and she would never be without a place to stay.

"I got a job selling papers, shining shoes, working in a grocery store, and doing all that I could to be the leader of my family. So I learned skills—leadership skills—early on in life because my mom was put on the street and I found a place for her to stay, and then worked for the people that owned the building."

An accomplished high school athlete, Little felt that his academics needed refinement to compete academically at the best colleges. "I went on to a military school (Bordentown Academy) and learned to do the necessary things that were important in terms of discipline, integrity, and character—all of those things that are intangibles."

Thanks to his efforts, Little earned a full scholarship to Syracuse, where he was given one of the ultimate honors in college football in the 1950s and '60s. Syracuse awarded him number 44, the number both Jim Brown and Heisman Trophy winner Ernie Davis had worn for the Orangemen.

Little fondly recalls the impact Davis made on him. "The first African-American to win the Heisman, he was the pillar of what I wanted to be and what my family wanted me to be. He was the picture of what you would want anybody to be. So having met with Ernie and having dialogue with him about Syracuse and what it meant to him, and what it helped him to become was enormous.

"Davis talked about Jim Brown and his influence on him. His obligation to replace Brown, and to replace himself with someone like me was inspiring."

At a time when freshmen could not play varsity football, Little became a three-time, consensus All-America running back at Syracuse,

Floyd "The Franchise" Little (44) played all nine seasons of his professional career with the Broncos, and his teammates chose him as their captain every year.
Courtesy of the Denver Broncos

the nation's first three-time All-America halfback since Doak Walker. He shattered the records that Davis and Brown had set at Syracuse and scored in all but eight games during his entire college career.

Drafted number one by the Denver Broncos in 1967, he became the first number-one draft choice to be signed by the team.

THE SETTING

The East Coast native recollects his reaction to the news of being drafted by Denver. "I was not happy. When Denver drafted me I was like, 'Where the hell is Denver?' I could not believe it when I got a call from (head coach) Lou Saban that they had drafted me to the Denver Broncos. I was like you have got to be kidding me. I could not believe it 'til I flew out here to meet Lou Saban. I was just amazed and fell in love with Denver the first day that I saw it."

And Denver fell in love with him right away. The first bona fide national superstar in Broncos history, Little was coming to a team and city hungry for success and an identity in pro football. Little would supply the cornerstone for building franchise respect by maintaining a sterling standard of play and a quality of leadership matched very few times since.

His status on the team and in the community was so revered that the five-time all-star was the team's only captain, as selected by his peers, during his entire nine-year career. His standard of excellence was such that any reasonable ranking of Bronco players would place him on the kind of list that can be counted on one hand.

"We had 26 rookies on our team that first year, and it is very difficult to compete on the level of the National Football League with 26 rookies—half of all the players. But the fans were so supportive and so loyal that they came out and they supported us, and every time that I got on the field I wanted to perform for them. They were the world's greatest fans because we were never disappointed by their support," Little remembers.

Sometimes those fans went to Broncos games with only The Franchise to cheer for. Dismal season followed dismal season until the

FLOYD LITTLE AT A GLANCE

POSITION: Running Back
COLLEGE: Syracuse University
PLAYING HEIGHT, WEIGHT: 5-10, 196
YEARS PLAYED FOR BRONCOS: 1967-75
UNIFORM NUMBER: 44 (retired)
NOTABLE: An inductee into the first class (1984) of the Denver Broncos Ring of Fame, Floyd Little is one of the greatest running backs in pro football history. A Hall of Fame candidate who was named by his teammates as the Broncos' team captain all nine of his seasons in pro ball, he was named to the league all-star team five times in his nine campaigns. The Broncos' record book features his name in virtually every significant category for a running back. Little retired as the seventh all-time leading rusher in NFL history, and led the NFL in total rushing yards from 1968-73. He was also first in yards from scrimmage during that six-year timeframe. The Pro Football Hall of Fame Selection Committee named Little to the All-Pro team of the 1970S. Among numerous off-field honors, Little won the 1974 Byron White Humanitarian Award presented by the NFL Players Association. He was inducted into the Colorado Sports Hall of Fame in 1977.
THE GAMES: Cleveland at Denver, October 29, 1972; Philadelphia at Denver, December 14, 1975

first winning campaign in 1973, Little's seventh year as a pro. Since that time, no team has had fewer losing seasons than the Broncos.

During Little's exemplary career, he tallied a team-record 12,173 all-purpose yards (a record that would last for more than 30 years). He led the NFL in rushing during the 1971 season with 1,133 yards after having led the American Football League in rushing in 1970. He remains the only halfback in history to be the leading rusher in different leagues in consecutive seasons.

"I just enjoyed playing so much for those fans that were more knowledgeable than any fans in the National Football League, said

Little. "But more importantly, they were more supportive of their team and its players."

And so it happened that the Broncos celebrated Floyd Little Day at Mile High Stadium on October 29, 1972.

THE GAMES OF MY LIFE

"It was amazing for me," Little recalls. "The fans that had come out were a sellout, of course—the Broncos have sold out every game since 1969, and I am very proud to have had a role in the beginning of that fantastic record. There were so many gifts, and so much heart and soul behind the gifts themselves.

"There was a boat donated by the Chrysler dealers. The Chevrolet people that I had been doing some promotional work for had a Blazer out there with my name on the side and my number on the side. All the fans had donated a lot of things to the Boys and Girls Club for whom I had served on the Board of Directors. For those fans to come out on a cold day and have all of those people there, it was so outstanding. They were hollering and screaming. I got a letter from the president of the United States, Richard Nixon, and a letter from the governor. The mayor had proclaimed it Floyd Little Day. For me as a player and for our developing city, it was just huge. Just absolutely huge and so emotional—my emotions were just out of control."

The factor that made this day more unusual is that it did not even come at the end of Little's career. Usually if a player has a "day" it is at the end of his career. The unabashed love that cascaded down onto No. 44 was made all the more astonishing since it happened while Little was still in his prime. "I had only played five years and I was receiving all of these accolades and all of these things from the governor, the mayor, and the president of the United States. It was standing room only at the game."

The Broncos had enjoyed great success against Cleveland, and in Little's era they had defeated the Browns the year before, and would beat them again the year after. But on Floyd Little Day, the visitors

Denver honored Floyd Little and his 1971 NFL rushing title on October 29, 1972, by celebrating Floyd Little Day at Mile High Stadium. His family was on hand for the ceremony. *Courtesy of the Denver Broncos*

drove for a game-winning touchdown with less than three minutes to play. It was 27-20, Browns.

Little had scored on a 19-yard, third-period reception to give Denver the lead, but the fledgling Broncos could not hold on. He carried 14 times for 79 yards, caught three passes and returned two punts, accounting for 118 total yards against Cleveland, but the fiercely competitive Little had to leave the field disappointed.

"That game to me was representative of how fans can absolutely embrace one of their own and express what they thought of him and his efforts and commitment. I was so happy to have taken the opportunity to come to a city with which I was unfamiliar, and embrace the people, the fans. That day was just for me. Every time I think about it, it is the thing that causes my emotional dam to break."

After the Broncos gave him his day, Little played three more seasons. In 1975 his career was coming to an end. The Broncos would finish a disappointing 6-8, and the home finale against the

Philadelphia Eagles on December 14 was widely known to be Floyd Little's last home game.

He reminded the fans one last time why they loved him so much, and he let the fans know that the feelings were completely mutual.

"Football was a great opportunity for me to learn life's lessons—a lot of life's lessons. I played it for the better part of my life, and I can remember seeing the last two minutes of the game on the clock as I stood there at the Philadelphia game, my last home game, and realizing that all of the things that I had been a part of as an athlete were going to end in two minutes. That was one hellacious time for me to look up at the clock and watch the end of an era for me tick away. I was thinking about life, and life after football.

"Life is about a lot of things. It is about living; it is about loving; it is about learning; it is about teaching. A lot of people do not know what their passion is in life. If you ask most people, 'What is your passion?' they don't know. We are born and we are given a certain grace when we are born, certain talents and skills that we have but we never know what they are because we never really pursued them. My passion always was to teach. I know that, that is what I am here for. The knowledge and experiences that I have gained in life, I have to pass that on. I can't take it with me, so I have been gathering all of this information to share with those who are interested and those who want to give it back. I don't want to take any knowledge with me when I leave. My passion in life is to give my knowledge freely and to teach accordingly and to share information. So life for me has just been a picture."

The Broncos beat Philadelphia by a score of 25-10, an altogether more fitting finale for Little than the Cleveland game three years earlier, and he was a huge factor in the Denver offense against the Eagles.

"That game was surreal. It was the end of my career as an athlete. The greatest thing was when guys like (Eagles linebacker) Bill Bergey and (Eagles wide receiver) Harold Carmichael during the game would say to me, 'Floyd, we are going to miss you. You are a great player; you helped to perpetuate this game of football that we all love. The guys who know and played against you know you were a fierce competitor, and we loved competing against you because you gave it your all and we are going to miss you.' Comments like that meant so much."

The final stats show 163 total yards for Little, still awfully good for a player on his way out, and he stopped at the exit door for one of the greatest last acts in Bronco history.

The game was tied at 10-10 in the third quarter, and Denver had the ball at its own 34-yard line. "I knew it was my last game, and I asked (quarterback) Steve Ramsey, 'Let's run a screen pass, because I am going to take it the distance,' and Ramsey called it. He threw the screen pass to me and I ran the yards being led by Haven Moses all the way down the sideline."

Little's hardest work on the play might have been the actual catching of Ramsey's high screen, which made the halfback leap completely off the ground to make the grab. "That wobbler! I had to catch one of Ramsey's wobblers. Then I had to do a lot of weaving, but I could see the path to the end zone, and the angles of the defenders worked well for me," he modestly recalls. It was the 53rd time he had reached the end zone as a Bronco, but it still was not the last.

"There was huge personal significance to that touchdown, because I scored the first time that I played in Bears Stadium (the Broncos' home before expansion and renaming by the city). So I scored in my first game as a Bronco, and I scored in my last game."

Denver added a field goal and then had a final offensive series in the final minutes of the game. It was a nine-play drive that included one reception and four runs by Little, the last one greatly anticipated by the adoring fandom. With the ball at the Philadelphia two, everyone knew the play, and Little was called upon to carry the ball one last time. He went in untouched with 1:56 to play for his second touchdown in the last home game.

"I came to the sidelines and watched the clock go down, and I was just flooded with thoughts and emotions.

"It was unbelievable. Some guys came out of the stands and carried me off of the field. I don't know how they got on the field. I can't even identify them. I wish that I could. They hoisted me up on their shoulders and they carried me off of the field. I really wanted to linger a little bit because that was the last time I would ever be on that field in that capacity. But they came out and off I went!

"Charlie Johnson (quarterback and fellow Ring of Famer) was waiting after the game at the locker room with a chauffeur's hat and a limousine to take me over to the party that my teammates had arranged for me with the coaches and their wives and everything. They had a big ice sculpture with my number on it and it was just an incredible way to end my career. But had I known that the Broncos were going to go to the Super Bowl that next year I would have hung on for another year."

AFTER THE CHEERING STOPPED

For Floyd Little, the playing stopped, but the cheering never did.

After his retirement he said, "One is always continuing the theme of leadership. Your life isn't over, you are just moving on, and a person has to continue to do things, to grow, develop, and contribute.

"Football has been a great teacher for me. The things that I learned from football and from my teammates have helped me to become a better person in life and in business. What you learn on a daily basis can certainly catapult you into your next career." He successfully parlays that knowledge as the owner and operator of a Ford dealership in Seattle.

Little was a member of the Denver Broncos' inaugural Ring of Fame class in 1984. The induction ceremony and every other visit has been punctuated by the unceasing cheers of Broncos fans who will never forget the days when The Franchise was just one player.

Syracuse University retired the number 44 in 2005, and all of the players who wore that illustrious number were there for the ceremony. Recalling the most vivid memory of that day, Little says, "They asked Jim Brown to speak on behalf of all the players who had worn the number, and Jim Brown referred to me. He said, 'Floyd Little was the greatest running back who ever wore the number 44. He is the only three-time All-American in the history of this school. He should be the one to represent the number 44.' Can you imagine that? Jim Brown bowed to me.

"I have always tried to conduct myself with dignity and pride. My mom would not have wanted it any other way. I don't care for some of the attitudes of some of the players today, but I think that we represent ourselves in such a way that we are role models whether we want to be or not. You never know who you will influence.

"I got to know Jim Gray, a longtime Denver resident and national TV reporter, and he got a star in the Hollywood Walk of Fame in 2005. I got a call from him asking me if I would be a part of that ceremony. Of course I said yes and then when he was on the podium to receive his award he said, 'I want to thank my hero, who is responsible for me being here. He is a person that I have looked up to so much, I wore his jersey every night as a boy.' And then he turned to me. I was just shocked, stunned, and amazed. And he said, 'I slept in it every night and my parents said, "Let us wash this jersey, he is just a football player." And Jim Gray said he told them, 'He is not just a football player. He is my hero and my idol and the person that I look up to, and I want Floyd Little to know that he is responsible for me being here.' I was just blown away."

Rare is the player of whom it can be said that the city gained more from him than he from the city.

Chapter 2

FRANK TRIPUCKA

BEFORE THE BRONCOS

There are many stories in sports about a team doing a favor for a player, giving him a chance to have a career, but Frank Tripucka's time with the Broncos represented the exact opposite, a player, indeed a retired player in this case, giving the team a chance.

The Broncos were the epitome of a ragtag operation when they began in 1960, and Frank Tripucka had already concluded a fine playing career and was about to give his full-time attention to the business world.

A star at Notre Dame in the 1940s and a first-round draft choice by the Philadelphia Eagles in 1949, Tripucka had played in the NFL and in Canada from then until 1959, and he had had enough. "I was playing up in Saskatchewan, and I figured it was about time I quit because I was getting a little old then," he remembers.

But then he got a phone call.

"I had known (Broncos head coach) Frank Filchock up in Canada and I also knew (Broncos general manager) Dean Griffing up in

Canada," Tripucka relates. "So I came home and the next thing you know I get a call from Dean Griffing who said they were starting a team out in Denver and he wanted to know if I could help out with the coaching. So I said, 'Sure, I'd be happy to come out there, for a couple of weeks anyway.'"

A couple of weeks?

"I went out to Golden to the Colorado School of Mines, next thing I knew they were playing an intra-squad game later on the first week. So, I was sitting there on the sideline, and Filchock said to me, 'These people aren't getting their money's worth. How about you going in the second half and throwing a couple of passes. At least give them their $5 worth.' I said, 'Yeah, I'd be happy to.' So I went in the second half and stayed in for four more years."

The early Broncos were ragtag in ways that one cannot even imagine. The budget was limited, the uniforms were used—mustard and brown, with vertically striped socks that became so legendary for their hideousness that a pair today resides in the Pro Football Hall of Fame.

Tripucka, dubbed "The Tripper" by sportswriters in his day, recalls, "Griffing was on a very limited budget. He was a cheap guy to start with and he didn't spend a buck if he didn't have to. Those uniforms, he ended up buying them from some minor-league team out on the West Coast. That's how we ended up with those brown-striped socks with the brown pants and the mustard (home) and white (road) jerseys."

In fact, had it not been for a national television contract, the American Football League certainly would not have stayed afloat long enough to be part of today's NFL.

So on the cusp of retirement from pro football, this is the assignment Tripucka voluntarily took upon himself as a favor to old friends in 1960. The Broncos lost and lost big for two years, with the

---

Quarterback Frank Tripucka was one of the original Denver Broncos and led the team to its first .500 record in 1962.
Courtesy of the Denver Broncos

old Notre Damer valiantly slinging the ball and trying to keep the Broncos in games while running for his life.

THE SETTING

Some things finally changed in 1962.

The Broncos brought Jack Faulkner in from San Diego to be the head coach. San Diego was a top-notch team in the league at that time. Faulkner brought with him the Broncos' first playbook, and the team designed new uniforms, choosing orange as the main color without realizing how prominent it would become in the Mile High City.

Prior to 1962 the Broncos had always opened on the road due to the minor-league baseball team using Denver's Bears Stadium (named for the baseball team). But Faulkner wanted the edge of opening at home, so in 1962 they took the unusual step of playing their home opener at the University of Denver Stadium. "The stadium just sat there empty," Tripucka notes, "since they did not play football any longer, so we ended up playing our opening game there and we ended up winning it against the Chargers, 30-21. So of course, everyone was just thrilled to death because all we ever did was lose before."

The Broncos had opened with a win, in their new orange uniforms.

"Faulkner was the one that came in and said, 'My God, you've got to do something about these uniforms. We put this team out there, and if you want them to play like a major-league team you've got to make them look like a major-league team!' So we ended up with the orange uniforms—orange jerseys, white pants with the blue piping on it. We looked like a million dollars!"

And the next week Denver took to the road to face Buffalo.

THE GAME OF MY LIFE

Reaching 2-0 was a very big deal for this bedraggled franchise, and the Broncos would have to do it in old War Memorial Stadium, where

FRANK TRIPUCKA AT A GLANCE

POSITION: Quarterback
COLLEGE: University of Notre Dame
PLAYING HEIGHT, WEIGHT: 6-2, 192
YEARS PLAYED FOR BRONCOS: 1960-63
UNIFORM NUMBER: 18 (retired)
NOTABLE: A 1986 inductee into the Denver Broncos Ring of Fame, Frank Tripucka was one of the original Broncos. He led the team to its first .500 record (7-7 in 1962), and threw for 51 touchdowns as a Bronco. His 447 yards passing against Buffalo (September 15, 1962) stood as the team record for 38 years, and he shares the team record for most touchdown passes in a game with five (October 28, 1982 vs. Buffalo). Tripucka played in the AFL All-Star Game in 1962. He was inducted into the Colorado Sports Hall of Fame in 1983.
THE GAME: Denver at Buffalo, September 15, 1962

30,577 showed up to watch an AFL known for wide-open offensive football.

Tripucka did not disappoint them. The old passer, who two and a half years ago had gone into that intra-squad game to "give them their money's worth," proceeded to have the game of his life against the Bills, on his way to a season that would end with Tripucka playing in the AFL All-Star Game.

The Broncos could not run the ball much, or well, in those early days, so all hopes were pinned on Tripucka's arm. He eventually completed 29 of 56 passes against the Bills for a staggering 447 yards and two touchdowns.

But it didn't start off easy for Tripucka or the Broncos.

Denver managed only a field goal in the first half and trailed by a 20-3 margin at the break.

"We just kept passing, even though they knew that's what we had to do. There were not a lot of options for us at that time but I told the guys that as long as they kept blocking and catching, I'd keep throwing. At least we had plays to run against Buffalo. In the first two years of operation we did not have a playbook at all, so I would draw up the plays in the dirt in the huddle, and just look for whoever I thought would be open," Tripucka recalls.

In the second half, Tripucka flipped a touchdown pass to another former Notre Damer, wide receiver Bob Scarpitto, who had six catches for 90 yards that day. Fellow Ring of Famer Lionel Taylor caught nine for 133 yards.

Of Taylor, Tripucka says, "He was far and away the greatest receiver I've ever played with. We used to draw the plays on the ground. We'd get in the huddle, I would draw, and Lionel would say, 'I can do this to this guy and that to that guy.' I'd say, 'OK, let's go.'"

Of course, the Broncos had a playbook against the Bills, but Tripucka never lacked for improvisational skills. "At that time, you've got to realize that all these AFL teams played man for man, there was no such thing as zone coverage. Everybody played man for man. If you had a good guy running patterns it was for a reason—Lionel Taylor could run a pattern and I knew him like a book and that was it. That's where we became successful."

But the big play of the day came in the fourth quarter and was a combination of playbook, end-zone daring, and the improvisational speed of a young receiver named Al Frazier. It produced the game-tying touchdown and a new record for the fledgling league.

Tripucka's offense had been pushed back to Denver's four-yard line with just over seven minutes left in the game, and the old signal caller was facing an extraordinarily improbable third-and-36 situation.

With his team down by a score, The Tripper fired a 96-yard touchdown pass to Frazier, one of the biggest plays of his or anyone's career. "Like I said, we just kept slinging the ball. And Frazier could fly," Tripucka humbly notes.

That 96-yard touchdown pass was the longest play from scrimmage in early AFL history, and it remains the longest play ever made if considering the number of yards needed just for the first down.

Tripucka engineered one final drive, this one coming in the game's final moments. He passed the Broncos to the Buffalo three-yard line, where placekicker Gene Mingo nailed the game-winning field goal with 25 seconds remaining.

"I played a lot of years, and threw a lot of footballs," says Tripucka. Those 447 passing yards stood as a Bronco record for 38 years, surviving even the 16-year career of Hall of Fame quarterback John Elway.

Frank Tripucka's number 18 jersey was retired by the Broncos upon the end of his Denver career, a career which had begun with The Tripper doing a favor for a couple of old friends.

AFTER THE CHEERING STOPPED

The Tripuckas stayed in New Jersey after his playing days ended, and Frank was finally able to embark full time on that business career.

He first got into the liquor business as owner of a liquor store and then got wind of a beer distributorship up in Patterson that was available for him to buy. He did so and built it up from a four-truck business to a 20-truck operation. "I was very fortunate. That was about the time that Miller came out with Miller Lite. So I was pretty lucky that I had this Miller franchise and they were coming out with Miller Lite, and prior to that Miller never came east. It was strictly a midwestern beer until they came east, and since then everything has been history. It's become the second largest brewery in the country."

The self-deprecating Tripucka never points out that people make their own luck, or that the harder he worked, the luckier he got, but there is no question he enjoyed great success in the business world.

"I am basically retired now. I piddle around with the Central Plastics Company. I own it but my daughter-in-law runs the show. She's an engineer." There are six boys in addition to the daughter, and the Tripuckas enjoy watching the activities of their grandchildren.

His pro football career, which began in 1949, enjoyed its exclamation point when Broncos owner Pat Bowlen named Tripucka to the team's Ring of Fame in 1986.

"I was just thrilled to death. Being in the Broncos Ring of Fame and being one of only three players to have their number retired (John Elway's number seven and Floyd Little's number 44 are the other two), that is quite an honor.

"I had already been dabbling in business back in 1960, but I wanted to go out and help my old friends Frank Filchock and Dean Griffing for just a couple of weeks; it turned out to be a blessing in disguise, and I was thrilled to death with how it all turned out."

Chapter 3

RANDY GRADISHAR

BEFORE THE BRONCOS

Randy Gradishar is the poster boy for character, leadership, and family values.

Everything about Gradishar's story would seem corny, if it were not all true. The prototypical All-American boy, he literally was raised in Champion, Ohio, before matriculating to Ohio State. Legendary coach Woody Hayes called him "the best linebacker I ever coached at Ohio State." No small praise from as stern a taskmaster as Hayes was known to be.

Of course, Gradishar was a three-year starter for the Buckeyes and was named to every All-America team following his senior season as well as being an Academic All-American.

But just being from a place called Champion did not give Gradishar a free pass to greatness.

"I've always looked at athletics as basic fundamentals," says Gradishar. "And basic fundamentals means a lot of different things— whether it's running sprints, whether it's lifting weights, whether it's playing in a game, whether it's practicing. For 17 years of my life it always came back to basic fundamentals."

What went into creating a player of Gradishar's caliber? He explains, "There is the God-given talent that people have, and the rest of it is work. Then you get involved with the word 'commitment.' Committed to being the best I can be. I wanted to be a winner; I wanted to be a leader. I didn't want to be a follower."

The Ohio State and Broncos star believes that his value system didn't change much going as far back as his freshman year in high school. "I always liked the characteristics and traits of being a leader. You think of the word 'accountability,' you think of the word 'discipline,' you think of the word 'respect.' Having team goals, having individual goals, having a vision for yourself, those things were all really important to me."

No one who plays competitive athletics ever knows how far he is going to go, but Gradishar embodied the concept of success. "I wanted to be the best I could be. That doesn't mean that I am necessarily the number-one NFL, college, or high school player that Ohio ever had or the Denver Broncos have ever had, but from a personal standpoint I know that I gave it my best. I gave it 110 percent in those characteristics of character, commitment throughout life on the field and off the field."

Young Gradishar was a coach's dream, embodying all the virtues of team and small-town America. An obvious number-one draft choice, he was an immediate pick by Broncos coach John Ralston when Denver's turn came. Ralston had begun to turn the Broncos around, and Gradishar was "not a player you could pass up," according to his first pro coach.

Gradishar came to Denver and was an integral piece of the puzzle as the Broncos went from a laughingstock team to a respectable one, to a very good one that finally reached the Super Bowl in that 1977

Randy Gradishar played the game of his life against Cleveland on October 5, 1980, bearing the pain of torn rib cartilage and of losing his father four months earlier.
Rod Hanna/Denver Broncos

dream season. And because Gradishar was no less than a great player, he was a starter, an all-star, and the league's most valuable player. But his values were what drove him, and that value system gave him a perspective far beyond wins and losses.

How he was raised, and where he was raised, combined to set up the game of his life when he least expected it.

THE SETTING

When the Broncos played the Browns on October 5, 1980, it was not for a championship, but rather was just another early-season NFL game. But personal events were setting a special stage for Randy Gradishar.

It was 1980, the sixth year of Gradishar's illustrious career, and by then the Orange Crush defense had led the Broncos to the 1977 Super Bowl, and the Broncos' middle linebacker was recognized as one of the game's finest defenders. By any standard, he was one of the leaders on that defense.

His father had died in June of 1980 of an aneurism. The Broncos would play in Cleveland that season, and the connections affected the young linebacker to a high degree. He had grown up near the Browns' Hiram training camp.

"When my father passed away in June, I thought about it coming back from the funeral from Ohio to Denver. It never really left my mind. I already knew what the schedule was, and I knew we would be going back to Ohio for that game in October."

The week leading up to the game was mentally full for him.

"Many times people do not think of football players as regular guys with emotions and feelings, because we certainly keep those things to ourselves. And that whole week of practice the feelings kept coming out. We were traveling on Saturday and playing on Sunday, and I kept remembering how my father and I used to go to Cleveland Browns games and Cleveland Indians games at the Cleveland Municipal Stadium, and I knew that this time my father wouldn't be there."

RANDY GRADISHAR AT A GLANCE

POSITION: Linebacker
COLLEGE: The Ohio State University
PLAYING HEIGHT, WEIGHT: 6-3, 233
YEARS PLAYED FOR BRONCOS: 1974-83
UNIFORM NUMBER: 53
NOTABLE: Randy Gradishar was a seven-time Pro Bowler for Denver and is the Broncos' all-time tackles leader with 2,049 over his 10-year career. Gradishar played in every game of his career (145 consecutive) and accounted for 33 turnovers (20 interceptions and 13 fumble recoveries). He was voted Defensive Player of the Year in 1978 (AP, UPI, Pro Football Weekly, and NEA). The Denver Broncos inducted him into the Ring of Fame in 1989, the College Football Hall of Fame followed suit in 1998, and he has been a finalist for induction into the Pro Football Hall of Fame. In 1987, Gradishar was inducted into the Colorado Sports Hall of Fame.
THE GAME: Denver at Cleveland, October 5, 1980

The Broncos arrived in Cleveland on Saturday the day before the game, and Denver's All-Pro defensive leader had asked for a single room that week. He did not want a roommate on this trip. "On Saturday night I ordered a meal in my room, and I did not sleep well at all, waking up all night long."

He tried to maintain his game-day routine, going to chapel services, trying to talk with his teammates about the game. "My emotions were running overboard. Plus, we had just lost a game on Monday night against New England and, of course, (head coach) Red Miller was hotter than hot because we'd just been embarrassed on a Monday night game. The pressure was on. We had to play better; we had to beat the Browns. So as a leader, I felt lots of additional pressure, which nobody knew.

"I hadn't explained anything to anybody. I didn't talk about that to any players or coaches. On Sunday morning I was kind of crying, just feeling overwhelmed with these emotions. I certainly didn't feel like playing in any football game, or like being a leader, or some guy that is going to go out there and change the game."

The Broncos arrived in the decaying locker room at Cleveland Stadium, and fellow linebacker and soulmate Tom Jackson could tell something was amiss. Jackson finally asked, "Randy, what's wrong with you?"

Gradishar put up a good front for his teammates, but realized that he wasn't fooling them. "I was just different in a lot of ways—emotionally, mentally—and I guess it was apparent in my actions and behaviors. The bottom line is that I didn't even feel like playing. I was trying to convince myself and praying that the Lord would help me to go out and be able to play the game and play the best that I could."

He went through the pregame warm-up in the rote manner of someone who has been playing the game for years, but his heart was nowhere near Cleveland.

THE GAME OF MY LIFE

When the game began, there was only one way Randy Gradishar ever knew how to play. He played like he was the most significant player on the field, and oftentimes he was.

The game was a defensive battle that featured seven field goals, three by Cleveland kicker Don Cockroft, a Colorado native, and four by the Broncos' Fred Steinfort, who connected from 18, 47, 41, and 19. There was only one offensive touchdown in the game, on a second-quarter pass by Cleveland quarterback Brian Sipe.

Just before halftime the Browns held a 10-6 lead, and Sipe had driven the Browns from their own 23 to the Denver one on a beautiful 15-play drive.

It was third and goal at the one, with the Browns looking for some cushion on the scoreboard between themselves and the Broncos. As Gradishar remembers, "I felt the pressure of losing last week, the pressure of Red Miller, the pressure of (defensive coordinator) Joe Collier, besides that of an individual player trying to do a good job playing the best I could."

Denver was in its short-yardage defense at the one, with the Browns getting ready to score. At that point one of the most inexplicable plays in Broncos history took place.

The Broncos' middle linebacker was focused in his short-yardage stance. Sipe took the snap, and Gradishar tells the rest in present tense, as though it is happening still: "Tom Jackson blitzes in from the outside as he always does, creates havoc. Sipe throws the ball. I tip it and it ends up back down to the ground. But Tommy is lying on the ground on his back, and the ball literally never hits the ground; instead it bounces off Tommy's chest back into my arms. I immediately start running and the referee (Jerry Seeman) is right there running with me, so I knew it was good."

But Gradishar and Seeman were the only people heading downfield. It happened so quickly—virtually all the players on both sides thought the ball had hit the ground—that no one else was running. Gradishar headed 93 yards for a touchdown ("I probably just kind of lumbered"), with the game referee as his only convoy.

That 93-yard touchdown put Denver ahead by a 13-10 margin. Both teams played tough second-half defense, and the Broncos held on for a grim 19-16 win. But one play made the day.

And, unbeknownst to him, Gradishar made his run while injured. But never one to make a big deal of injuries, he played through it. "Some big offensive lineman fell on me in the first half, and I ended up cracking cartilage in my rib. I went over and got Ace bandaged up, because I couldn't breathe very well. Eventually they figured out that I tore cartilage off of my rib cage. So I had that pain, and the pain of my father's death."

He had gone from, as he describes it, "the lowest part of my career as an athlete," to a 93-yard, game-changing touchdown that still stands in the Denver record books as the longest regular-season interception return. "I remember looking back and everyone was just kind of standing there. Then I looked at the film on Monday and no one was chasing me. I bounced and nobody reacted to it. I really believe that it wasn't luck but through my faith. I believe that that was a blessing for me. And an example of how God can take the worst circumstance and make that a blessing. Even though it was part of winning a game, it's part of a blessing."

An amusing aside, Seeman was the Big 10 referee who kicked Gradishar out of the Ohio State-Michigan game his sophomore year. "Every time I would see Jerry Seaman I would always go up and thank him for throwing me out of the Michigan game my sophomore year up in Ann Arbor," Gradishar recalls with laughter.

Very active in team chapel activities throughout his career, he tied the play, and the day, to his faith. "By faith you think that God is going to give you the opportunity to at least play, and play at the best you can. There is something you don't see and it turns out that at the lowest point, personally and for the team, you get a 93-yard interception for a return and we end up winning the game. So, that's part of my faith."

Gradishar often recites a favorite Bible passage from Hebrews 11:1, "Faith is the assurance of things hoped for, with the evidence of things not yet seen."

AFTER THE CHEERING STOPPED

When his playing career ended, he stayed in Denver, and every type of work he has thrown himself into projects a positive influence on people and personalities.

After playing for the Broncos, he directed the Denver Broncos Youth Foundation for eight years and worked with non-profit youth organizations.

Family, work and community always have been paramount to Gradishar. He is married (Beth), has three kids, a job, and charity involvement that seems like a full-time job in itself.

Currently he is the director of corporate communications with the Phil Long Dealership Group, which has 17 stores in Denver, Colorado Springs, and Pueblo. The dealership has 1,300 employees, making it the largest privately held auto retailer in Colorado. Gradishar is always available to extend his positive influence to every one of their employees, but his biggest impact is through that group's community fund, granting money to non-profit youth organizations, through their vehicle sales. A charity partner with Denver Broncos Charities, his organization has built nine fantasy playgrounds—five in Denver and four in Colorado Springs.

He has also maintained a significant involvement with the military. "Two years ago I had an opportunity to visit Kuwait and Baghdad. A year ago I was in Afghanistan and Qatar, thanking our troops. The Phil Long Group has always been involved with the community, so it's an opportunity to pay it forward."

People often talk about paying back to the community, but Gradishar says, "I prefer to pay it forward. After having had a great career with the Broncos and being involved in the community, I want to continue to pay forward.

"Colorado and the Broncos have always been great to me and for me, and I hope that over my 32 years here in Colorado I have been an asset for them as well."

Chapter 4

ED McCAFFREY

BEFORE THE BRONCOS

One of the most popular players in franchise history, Ed McCaffrey is one of the few Broncos ever to be serenaded by his own chant, as "E-D-D-I-E" would often cascade through Mile High Stadium after yet another big catch. He was hardworking, intelligent, diligent, loyal, and true—a coach's dream with great hands and deceptive speed.

And he was very, very competitive. "I'll have to admit that I've always been pretty competitive, and I'm not exactly sure why," McCaffrey said. "I was probably just born that way. I always loved sports. I love sports. I love to play sports, win or lose, but obviously winning was a whole lot more fun. I played football, basketball, and baseball as a kid. I had an affinity for just about every type of sport that's out there."

McCaffrey's childhood was spent in Allentown, Pennsylvania, where he played, grew, and learned great family values in the middle-class McCaffrey household, starring in football before getting a scholarship at Stanford.

He notes, "I was very fortunate to be able to play college football. There were several schools that were interested in having me play for their program. I visited a lot of incredible schools, but I absolutely fell in love with Stanford. At the time, it was the No. 1-ranked university in *U.S. News & World Report* academically, and academics were always extremely important to me. Football was always fun and I took it seriously, but it was always a game and I wasn't sure exactly how long I'd be lucky enough to play. But Stanford had a wonderful campus. They were an incredible academic institution that I thought I was very privileged to be able to attend. I thought going there greatly assisted my personal development, which in turn was a great part of my future development as a pro football player."

The New York Giants drafted him in the third round in 1991, but he never escaped being thought of as a backup player, and eventually was released.

"I always wanted to be a part of a championship-caliber team. In high school my junior and senior year, my team finished 0-11 and 2-9. In college, although we did get to one bowl game, that was it in my five-year stint at Stanford. So I felt incredibly lucky to be drafted by the Giants because they had just won the Super Bowl, and it was always really important for me to be on a successful team. So I looked at it as a wonderful opportunity to be a part of a championship team, something that I hadn't been part of in a long time."

But there was a head coaching change, with the accompanying change in philosophy and outlook on personnel. "Whenever there's a coaching change, coaches a lot of times go with players that they know of or that they've coached before, and that was what happened with me and the Giants," McCaffrey remembers. So it was on to the 49ers in 1994, where he thrived.

Wide receiver Ed McCaffrey played in three Super Bowls in his career—Super Bowl XXIX with the 49ers and Super Bowl XXXII and Super Bowl XXXIII with the Broncos.
© David Lissy/Rich Clarkson and Associates

"I absolutely think that my experience in San Francisco had a lot to do with my future success in the NFL. At some point throughout all the coaching changes and the adversity that I experienced in New York, I started taking football probably way too seriously, and some of the fun left the game for me. And when I had an opportunity to go to another team (from New York) there was a handful of teams who were interested in signing me, but I wanted to be with a team I thought had the chance to become a championship team."

He traveled to San Francisco and tried out with absolutely no guarantees. "They had a lot of really talented receivers, but at some point in that training camp, I feel like I just released all the pressure that I'd been putting on myself and started having fun again. I was catching footballs from Steve Young, and I was backing up Jerry Rice. I was going against Deion Sanders every day in practice with the second-team offense or sometimes the third-team offense. I had no idea whether I'd make it or not. But the thrill of competing and going against the best players in the league in practice was exhilarating to me, and about halfway through that training camp I just started having fun again. I didn't even care if I made the team. I thought, 'I have the opportunity to play today against the best DB in the league and catch balls from the best quarterback in the league.' That's a great opportunity, and I feel like once I allowed myself to have fun again I started becoming a better player."

The Niners continued to win, and the stars collided in the brightest of ways for McCaffrey, who was a valuable reserve on the championship team that featured Mike Shanahan as offensive coordinator.

"The San Francisco year was a whole lot of fun because I allowed myself to have fun again. Even though I wasn't a starter, I was a backup to the best receiver to ever play the game and I was playing on the best team in the world. I was having a whole lot of fun, even in practice. But I didn't get a whole lot of chances in the game. Fortunately, that team won the Super Bowl, and I actually was lucky enough to be in on a tackle on special teams and I got one catch in the Super Bowl game that we won pretty handily. But to me it was the thrill of a lifetime. I finally had the opportunity to become part of a Super Bowl

ED MCCAFFREY AT A GLANCE

POSITION: Wide Receiver
COLLEGE: Stanford University
PLAYING HEIGHT, WEIGHT: 6-5, 215
YEARS PLAYED FOR BRONCOS: 1995-2003
UNIFORM NUMBER: 87
NOTABLE: A starting wide receiver for the Denver Broncos in Super Bowl XXXII and Super Bowl XXXIII, Ed McCaffrey was also a member of a Super Bowl championship team with the San Francisco 49ers. He played in the Pro Bowl following the 1998 season, and was named All-NFL (Sports Illustrated) in 2000 and in 1998 (Associate Press second team).
THE GAME: Super Bowl XXXII, Denver vs. Green Bay, January 25, 1998, San Diego, California

championship team, and it ended up being one of the most fun years I've ever had," McCaffrey said, but his talent and personality drove him to want more.

A few days after San Francisco won the Super Bowl in 1994, Mike Shanahan got a new job with the Broncos, and McCaffrey was Denver-bound.

THE SETTING

The Broncos had gone to four Super Bowls—three with John Elway as quarterback and Mike Shanahan as an assistant coach—but the franchise had never won pro football's ultimate prize, and Shanahan returned to Denver with championship goals.

According to McCaffrey, "It was really a great opportunity for me. I didn't think, believe it or not, that Coach Shanahan even had much interest in signing me to the Broncos when he left and took the head coaching position, because I had barely played."

But one of Shanahan's coaching credos is that watching how a player practices is as important as watching how he plays. Shanahan said, "I watched McCaffrey practice every day, and I knew what kind of a special player Ed was and could be on Sunday, based on what he did during the week."

McCaffrey recalls it this way: "I think Mike probably thought to himself that, 'I don't know how good this player can be, but I know that he worked his butt off in practice every day and had fun and helped'—I hope, at least—'make our starters better players in San Francisco' by the way I would compete in practice. And I think that's the only way that he would've given me an opportunity to play in Denver. So although I like to think I was a little bit of a tough negotiator, I was jumping at the chance to get to play for Coach Shanahan in Denver and had no idea how much playing time I'd get. But he was offering me an opportunity to at least compete for a starting position. I thought the world of him as a coach because I had seen how he ran practices, how he game-planned and how he coached my year in San Francisco. It was a great opportunity to play for an incredible coach and have an opportunity to compete for some playing time.

"Mike gave me a chance to blossom, and he looks at it fairly. That is, he looks at the best players being out there."

Indeed, Shanahan wound up cutting two former number-one draft choices, Anthony Miller and Mike Pritchard, and going with relative unknowns McCaffrey and Rod Smith as his starting wide receivers. If Denver eyebrows had been raised any higher, they would have leaped off their respective heads.

"In the beginning of my career with the Broncos, I was a special teams player and a backup receiver. That's really where I met Rod and became close friends with Rod because we used to alternate at backup receiver, and they would hardly ever throw us the ball. So we used to have competitions to see who could knock down the most DBs in a game. Again, that was one of my most fun years ever in the NFL, when Rod and I were both backups competing with each other to see how many knockdowns we could get in the game. As a receiver, you obviously want the ball all the time, but we just understood our situation. We had to pay our dues and earn our time. We decided one way we're going to get noticed is by how hard we block in the running game, and it was fun for a lot of reasons.

"One, it was just a fun team to be on with great players and great coaches. Two, I started developing friendships with other players on the team—Rod being one of them—and having friendly competitions. So rather than one of those competitions where you're fighting for your job and you're looking at the other receivers as the enemy, this was a situation where we were friends. We were rooting for each other and competing with each other to make each other better. That's an unbelievable experience.

"We were coming together as a team. We were going from being 8-8 into being one of the best teams in the league the following year—but getting eliminated in the playoffs. We were a team that had finally over a couple of years grown together to become a Super Bowl championship team."

History is written on the field, not on paper, and the Broncos went 13-3 in 1996, just the second year of this new alignment, sustaining a crushing home loss to Jacksonville in the playoffs that year.

McCaffrey proved himself an absolutely vital component of the Denver offensive package, for both his pass-catching and blocking ability.

In 1997 they began where they had left off the previous year, making the playoffs as a wild card before marching through Jacksonville, Kansas City, and Pittsburgh to set up Super Bowl XXXII against the defending world champion Green Bay Packers.

Now McCaffrey would be returning to the Super Bowl, not as a reserve player who barely got to play, but as a pivotal player with the chance to prove himself.

THE GAME OF MY LIFE

"The Broncos were a big underdog, whatever that means, in the game against the Packers, but there wasn't that feeling within our team. Absolutely not. In fact, it was tough for everyone, probably especially Shannon Sharpe, to not express our confidence verbally. It was tough for everyone not to make any comments two weeks before the game because we absolutely planned on winning that football

game, and all we heard for two weeks was how we were 14-point underdogs, how we'd be lucky to keep it close. It got really hard to not say anything, but there was never any doubt in our minds from the first play to the last play that we were going to win that football game.

"You could sense it, and as the game went along, I think the fans could sense it as well.

"I had no question about it, no doubt about it. You just kept your mouth shut all week long. The fans and the press especially were eating up the praise that we were throwing at the Packers in the press conferences. We'd praise them and the press would run with it. But deep down inside, we couldn't wait to get onto the field. We were just chomping at the bit to start the game. The Packers were a great football team. I'll take nothing away from them. They're a heck of a team. But we were a heck of a team, too, and we knew it. We knew that we could beat them, and we planned on beating them. It worked. The plan worked."

Ed McCaffrey was all about toughness, blocking, and doing the little things that show up on the game film instead of on the stats sheets.

"I didn't have a lot of catches against the Packers, but that's not what it was about. We won the game as a team. I had two catches for 45 yards, but one of them was a 36-yard reception, which was a huge reception in the game. But I am proudest of the fact that I was blocking all day long for Terrell Davis, and our success with the running game was our key offensively."

McCaffrey's two catches both came on the same drive, a third-quarter possession that resulted in a Denver touchdown. His 36-yard and nine-yard receptions put the Broncos in position for a Terrell Davis touchdown, one of three for the star running back against the Pack. McCaffrey spent most the day delivering pounding hits as a

Ed McCaffrey looks for extra yardage on this 36-yard reception against the Packers in Super Bowl XXXII, the game of his life in which his best work was done as a blocker for Terrell Davis.
Rich Clarkson/Denver Broncos

blocker to support the 157 rushing yards that made Davis the Super Bowl MVP.

"Maybe the most 'famous' block of the game was the one in the winning fourth-quarter drive, captured by NFL Films. I really got excited over that block. Usually I just did my job and was not overly demonstrative, but that block was key as Terrell had a big carry around left end, and I just could not resist pointing to the defender after he was lying down. My emotions took over on that play."

Behind McCaffrey's blocks, Denver rushed for 79 yards in the first half, then came back for 100 more in the second.

"Like any other receiver in the league, I'd love for them to throw me the ball on every play. But it's always been more important for me to be a part of a great team. The thing that I think I craved the most was the respect of my teammates and my coaches. Your teammates and coaches know what happens on every play, and they can see who's working hard in the running game and in the passing game. So in the beginning of my career, the only way I got on the field—because they wouldn't throw me a whole lot of passes—was to work extremely hard in the running game. I figured, 'I'm going to contribute in some way to this football team.'

"If that meant being a great blocking receiver, then that's what I was determined to be. When I was on the field, I wanted to help the team, so I did everything I could to help the team. That carried throughout my career, and never more so than in championship games like that one. I would love the ball on every play, but the most important thing to me is that whatever opportunity I get in the game, I'm making the most of it. If that means blocking and opening up holes for the running backs, then I was more than happy to do that. I always stayed ready. Then when my number was called, I'd do my best to make a play in the passing game as well. I just knew that on a team with so much talent, I wasn't going to get the ball on every play, but when I got my chance, again, I tried to make the most of it.

"That Super Bowl was a reflection of that—for me and really everybody else. We were doing what was called for, not only for the whole game, but more significantly, one play at a time We had a lot of great players on our team. I always trusted Coach Shanahan to put our team in the best position to win. I knew that he was going to call plays that he thought would work. There might have been times where I was wide open running down the field, but somebody else was open and they got the ball. That's just how it goes. I think that one of the reasons that team was so special was our unselfishness. Everybody out there was playing for each other, and everyone out there put the team ahead of themselves. That's why we were able to win."

In the pantheon of Broncos football, McCaffrey was regarded as one of the toughest receivers and leading fan favorites of all time. The fans always respected that toughness, and never more than that day against Green Bay. "I never had a sign on my back that said, 'These are my values.' But in the way you approach the game, I think they saw it and appreciated it," McCaffrey says of the Denver fans.

"The Denver Broncos fans are the greatest fans in the world, bar none. All I ever wanted to do was go out and have fun and earn the respect of my coaches and teammates through my hard work in practice and on the field. I honestly never expected to be embraced. And I'm not speaking of just myself. I'm talking about all of the wonderful players we had on those Super Bowl teams. I never expected to be embraced the way we were embraced by the fans. I think the Denver Broncos fans are pretty savvy. I think they understand the game, and they respect hard work and dedication. Win or lose, I think Denver Broncos fans can tell when players are laying it on the line for each other and when they're giving everything they have to the game. I always tried to do that, and I think Denver Broncos fans are aware that not just myself, but Rod and John and Shannon and our O-line, who played so incredibly well over those years, and the defense… They see when players and teams are giving it everything they have out on the football field. We always tried to do that, and I think the fans embraced our team because of it.

"That win over the Packers was for everybody—players, coaches, city, fans. It meant everything to me.

"I think that's why Super Bowl XXXII was so special to me. Because I was there before, we just walked in and won a Super Bowl. I was there when the team was coming together, when the coaching staff was coming together. I was there for a couple of years while we worked together to become the best team that we could be. I saw the superstars, but also the role players who made sacrifices and were great players who maybe could have started on other teams, but stayed around to be part of something that was so special. That was even more special because it was the first Super Bowl championship for the Denver Broncos in their long history of great teams and Super Bowls. It just seemed like everything came together over a couple-of-year period and culminated in that one incredible game."

AFTER THE CHEERING STOPPED

Since retirement from pro football the ever-popular McCaffrey stayed in the Denver area. He and his wife, Lisa, are active in a variety of charitable concerns, while Ed has continued as a spokesman for local businesses.

For McCaffrey, family remains number one at all times. "I absolutely love to spend more time with my family. Lisa and I have four boys. I get to spend a lot more time with Lisa and my sons, and I help coach their football, basketball, and baseball teams. Before school and after school and weekends are pretty packed, but I absolutely love it. We're running all around the place, all around the state of Colorado, to different sporting events and extracurricular activities and helping with school. I get to be a big part of their lives.

"I loved playing in the NFL. It was absolutely a dream come true, and it ended up being more than I ever imagined, with memories I'll take with me throughout my entire lifetime. But one thing that I'm able to do now is be home on Saturdays and Sundays for the kids' games and take them to practice and help coach their teams. My kids are just at great ages, so I love being a part of their lives," he says, beaming with a father's joy.

Professionally, McCaffrey has always been driven by a need to stay engaged in lots of projects. And retirement from football is not retirement from working life.

"I think I'm just one of those people who always needs to be setting goals and working toward them, so I've worked for a couple of different companies. The company I'm working with now is a company called TIVIS Ventures. We're a private investment firm which helps to fund, manage, and grow new companies. It is really exciting to be part of something new, being on the ground floor of a company's growth."

Nothing can replace the excitement of playing in the NFL, he points out, but adds, "One thing that I am passionate about is being part of something from the beginning and helping to make it a success, as part of a team concept."

Just like Ed McCaffrey did in his football career.

Chapter 5

GOOSE GONSOULIN

BEFORE THE BRONCOS

Before Goose Gonsoulin, there were no Broncos. There are 187 trades listed in the Denver Broncos media guide from 1960 through 2005, and the trade for Gonsoulin was the first one Denver ever made.

Austin Gonsoulin was born and raised in Port Arthur, Texas, and he didn't start off life as "Goose." But he did start off as a player, like so many Texas kids. He was a high school star in Port Arthur, accepted a scholarship to Baylor University and there earned the attention of pro scouts, including Jack Faulkner of the Los Angeles Rams, who, unbeknownst to either man, would go on to coach Gonsoulin in Denver.

While at Baylor, the Texas native son named for the capital city was returning a punt, and assistant coach Hayden Fry called out the words of encouragement, "Come on, Goose." And thereafter Austin was known as Goose.

As a senior, Gonsoulin knew he would have a chance to play pro football and wanted to take a crack at it before settling into the business world.

He was drafted by the San Francisco 49ers of the NFL and by the upstart Dallas Texans of the new American Football league.

"Being a Texan, I wanted to stay in Texas. So I never even talked to the 49ers," he explains. "They offered me just over $8,000, so I took the money thinking that it was a guaranteed thing. There were a couple of bowl games coming up, including a Copper Bowl all-star game. I got the outstanding back of the game and had a good time."

Everything looked great for Gonsoulin. He was a native Texan getting set to play pro football in his home state. Then the Broncos made the first trade in team history, and acquired his rights from the Dallas Texans before any team in the AFL had even reported to training camp.

THE SETTING

If ever there was a ragtag outfit, it was the Denver organization to which Gonsoulin had been traded. He remembers thinking, "What am I going to do in that landlocked area up there in Denver? I like the coast a lot, and being somewhere in Texas for sure. This was very foreign to me."

He reported to camp on time, but was not prepared for the second-class nature of his new world. "When I arrived there were over 120 guys who'd been through the camp, there were truck drivers and all kinds of guys like that, not really many that were talented. We stayed in this huge gymnasium and the beds were all side by side."

But aside from the living arrangements, he still could count on the football itself being up to a certain standard, he thought.

In the game of his life against Kansas City on October 11, 1964, safety Goose Gonsoulin intercepted three of Len Dawson's passes, helping the Broncos finally claim a win over their rivals. *Courtesy of the Denver Broncos*

"Then I realized there were only three coaches, whereas our college team had about eight. The uniforms were all old and messed up. So we'd practice and play and there would be old Canadian and NFL guys coming through all the time for tryouts. I didn't know if we were going to make it. It was pretty easy to notice how tight the team was financially."

In fact, things were shaky enough financially for the new franchise that in 1960 Gonsoulin wasn't taking any chances. "We went on this road trip and stayed about five weeks, so I decided to bring all of my luggage with me because they were cutting guys on the bus, off the bus, in the dressing room. They'd take one guy off our bus and put him on another bus," he says, recalling it like a bad dream.

The Broncos were a miserable team in 1960, but Gonsoulin intercepted 11 passes and was an All-AFL selection, following that up with six interceptions in 1961. But you can't sugar coat the record. "It really was a nightmare. It was like we were playing for a semi-pro team.

"It was a rough time, and I couldn't believe that the fans kept coming out there. They were always great."

Gonsoulin had seven interceptions in 1962 and again made the AFL All-Star team, and he would do so again in 1963 with another six-interception season. But the Broncos had been big losers in the short history of the AFL. Original head coach Fran Filchock was fired after the 1961 campaign, and Jack Faulkner took the Broncos to a 7-7 mark in 1962, only to have the team regress in 1963, with Faulkner being fired the week the Broncos were about to play Kansas City in 1964.

THE GAME OF MY LIFE

Mac Speedie, who had been a great wide receiver for Otto Graham on the championship Cleveland Browns club, took over as head coach that week. The Broncos were about to play the Chiefs, the original Dallas Texans franchise that Gonsoulin thought he would be playing for in his home state.

GOOSE GONSOULIN AT A GLANCE

POSITION: Safety
COLLEGE: Baylor University
PLAYING HEIGHT, WEIGHT: 6-3, 210
YEARS PLAYED FOR BRONCOS: 1960-1966
NUMBER WORN: 23
NOTABLE: One of the four original inductees into the Denver Broncos Ring of Fame, Goose Gonsoulin was an All-American Football League selection in 1960, 1962 and 1963. At the end of his Broncos career he was the all-time AFL leader in pass interceptions with 43 and still ranks second in club history in that category. He shares the team and NFL record for interceptions in a game with four (September 18, 1960 at Buffalo). He was inducted into the Colorado Sports Hall of Fame in 1984.
THE GAME: Kansas City at Denver, October 11, 1964

Not only had the Broncos never beaten the franchise while they were in Dallas, going 0-6 over the first three years of play, but in 1963 the Texans became the Chiefs and pummeled the Broncos by scores of 59-7 and 52-21.

The misery was even more personal for Gonsoulin, who during his trips to the AFL All-Star game and met and become friendly with Kansas City quarterback Len Dawson.

"Len was, of course, one of the great players in the league, and would always kid me about our terrible record against his team. That would continue when we occasionally played golf. Sometimes Len and I would go out to dinner together the night before the game, and then go play each other the next day. So there was a real desire to do well against your friends."

The Chiefs had won the AFL title in 1962 and were still a very powerful team, while the Broncos were just trying to get a breath of fresh air, get organized, and keep the franchise afloat.

Gonsoulin remembers the week well. "Here we are trying to get better, but we're playing Kansas City, which has kicked our butts year after year. They wouldn't just kick it but run all over us, and the score would always be very lopsided."

The Broncos were fired up for their new coach and took a first-quarter 6-0 lead in the game. But in the second period, Dawson moved the Chiefs downfield, passing 14 yards to Chris Burford to give Kansas City a 7-6 edge.

On the next Chiefs possession, Gonsoulin recalls picking off a pass from his friend Dawson. "He threw the ball on a turn-in, but I overplayed it and came up with an interception."

Each team kicked two field goals to close out the half with the Chiefs ahead 13-12.

In the third quarter, Gonsoulin again picked Dawson off, this time returning the ball 24 yards to set up a Denver touchdown. "I remember walking by Len as we left the field, and he sort of playfully said, 'Hey you SOB, what are you doing to us?' We ran around together during those all-star games and were friends and all, but we were very competitive, and this was the first game when we were finally beating them."

Then in the fourth quarter the Denver safety picked off his friend for the third time, a theft that once again led to a Broncos score and an eventual 33-27 win, Denver's first over the Kansas City franchise. "Everybody was all excited because it was our first win over them. We were all pumped up. That was really special for the Broncos to do that because the Chiefs had real talent throughout.

"That was a big turning point for us and Denver fans really loved it. That day was really special for the Broncos organization and me."

AFTER THE CHEERING STOPPED

"Being a Bronco is still very, very important to me," he says anytime his career is mentioned. "After leaving Denver and going to the 49ers, I started at safety and felt good about that too, because I was one of the first players in the AFL to go up and make the NFL. I felt proud and I hope that the Denver fans felt proud, too."

When Gonsoulin's playing career ended he worked in Gulf Coast industrial sales for about a decade, then bought a 300-employee construction company. He held on to that for eight years, then got back into sales and was on the board of directors for a couple of banks and other ventures.

He remains modest about his success, but on being pressed acknowledges that his construction company had as many as 1,500 employees and did a lot of big construction jobs in the Gulf Coast region.

In 1984, long after his playing days ended, Gonsoulin got perhaps the most shocking phone call of his football-related career. It was Broncos owner Pat Bowlen calling to tell him he had been named to the inaugural class of the team's Ring of Fame.

"Oh my God, I was never so shocked in all of my life," he recalls.

A regular attendee at the team's annual alumni reunion dinner, he and his old buddies from the 1960s remember the rough years. "We just shake our heads at what's going on now compared to what went on back then; it's just amazing. It lifts us up, after what we went through back then—those were some hard times."

Despite his many commercial successes, Gonsoulin beams with his attachment to the Broncos' successes that came after his departure. "It makes you proud to be recognized for being part of the team's foundation. Now when I go around and say I'm an ex-Bronco it really has meaning.

"The thing that I am most proud of is being the last original Bronco to still be on the team. I'm the last one that they released from that original bunch. And at those Ring of Fame dinners, many times they call me up first. I feel SO special, for them treating me that way."

Now completely retired, Goose spends his time watching his four grandchildren, all of whom live nearby.

Chapter 6

RED MILLER

BEFORE THE BRONCOS

Like the Broncos themselves, Red Miller grew up hard.

He was born in 1927, right at the beginning of the Great Depression. He was one of 10 kids at the toughest financial time in the century for America. Miller recalls, "My dad was a coal miner, who could neither read nor write because he was pulled out of first grade and put in the coal mines. But he was tough and he was a worker. My mom was the same because to bring 10 kids up in that environment was tough. We had no money. We had no indoor water. No electricity. No heat, other than what we could get from wood or coal."

To call his a tough life is an understatement. He credits his parents and four older brothers for helping shape his childhood. "My mom was instrumental in guidance of spirituality and she was a believer in God and she was a great woman," he is quick to say.

"You never admitted failure or never cried because your brothers wouldn't let you. You got tough because of all of the work you had to do." So he commenced working every day of his life, as a shoeshine boy, a ditch digger, a cornhusker—anything that involved hands and backbone.

He developed an early love of football by watching nearby Western Illinois play. "It just took hold of me because I wanted to be tough. My brothers wanted me to be tough and I wanted to show them." By the fifth grade he was playing against tough kids in the neighborhood, mostly sons of coal miners showing off their grit. Just kids playing on dirt.

But it was obvious young Miller was different early.

He knew he loved the game and started reading books, going to the library to find out more about football. His desire to learn about the game proved insatiable.

There are watershed moments for many individuals as they find out what they want their lives to be, and young Robert Miller had his in the fifth grade.

"I had never been up in front of the classroom in grade school at that time. The teacher said everyone had to learn a poem that meant something to them and recite it before the class. It was hard for me, but I got up there and this is my poem, it's kinda corny, but it's right to the point:

It Couldn't Be Done
by Edgar A. Guest

Somebody said it couldn't be done
But he with a chuckle replied
That "maybe it couldn't," but he would be one
Who wouldn't say so 'til he tried.
So he buckled right in with a trace of a grin
On his face. If he worried, he hid it.
He started to sing as he tackled the thing
That couldn't be done, and he did it!

Head coach Red Miller—a man known for his fiery style and matching hair—shares his thoughts with a referee.
© Rich Clarkson and Associates

"It was a hard beginning, but it showed you how to live right and work hard. None of my family knew anything about sports because they had to work. In fact, none of them ever got to see me play, never once. I got to my senior year and went to the opportunities advancement program. I said, 'Sir, I don't want to waste your time, but I know what I want to do.' He looked at me and said, 'What's that?' I said, 'I want to be a football coach and I'm going to be the best.' That's what I told him. He kind of snickered. Anyway, that's how my love for it began."

A fine player at Macomb High School, Miller was team captain and all-state, then went to Western Illinois and was named most-valuable player three years in a row as a middle linebacker and an offensive guard.

He desperately wanted to be something, to be somebody, and he began the arduous climb up the small college coaching ranks, fighting the battle for every new opportunity until he became an assistant coach in the new American Football League in 1960. From then on, he would have steady employment in pro football as an assistant with a number of teams. By then the fiery redhead had become just "Red" to all who knew him.

Included in his experiences as an assistant was a stint with the Denver Broncos from 1963 through 1965. So he knew firsthand what "bad" really could mean.

His career progressed to being offensive coordinator of the New England Patriots in 1976, until the next year when the Broncos were ready for a change from John Ralston to someone who had the reputation of being a fierce leader. Broncos general manager Fred Gehrke had been a personnel man for the Broncos when Miller was an assistant a decade earlier, and Gehrke called Miller as soon as the job was open.

THE SETTING

The whole city was ready for a change when he got the job. Miller went to every banquet, talked to every group, and he brought with him a fervent enthusiasm that was contagious. The players, staff, and

RED MILLER AT A GLANCE

POSITION: Coach
YEARS COACHED FOR BRONCOS: 1977-1980 as head coach; 1963-1965 as assistant coach
NOTABLE: Red Miller was head coach of the Denver Broncos for the team's first Super Bowl appearance (Super Bowl XII following a 12-2 1977 season). He directed the Broncos to the AFC Championship in 1977, to AFC Western Division titles in 1977 and 1978, and to a wild-card playoff berth in 1979. Miller was the unanimous choice as NFL Coach of the Year for that 1977 season. He was inducted into the Colorado Sports Hall of Fame in 1988.
THE GAME: Oakland at Denver, January 1, 1978

entire city quickly picked up on the fact that there was a new coach in town, and Broncomania was about to explode onto the national scene.

"What I thought was lacking was team spirit and a team approach. When I went through the ranks, I took lots of notes and had books of notes on what to do and what not to do as a head coach because that's what I wanted to do. I thought we could win and we could win my way. That's the way I approached it."

Miller knew how hard it would be for a franchise to get over the hump and beat good teams in key games, because the consistent winners had been there and done that before. "We had the toughest rated schedule of any team, going into the season."

Red Miller's 1977 Broncos started the season 6-0 and never looked back. They raced through the AFC West and dropped just two games all year: a meaningless contest at Dallas on the season's final day; and an annual home-field loss at the hands of the Raiders, who had not lost in Denver since 1962.

The city was on fire with emotion for a team that had never made a trip to the playoffs in its entire history, led by a spirited coach whose hair itself evoked an image of orange. People painted their cars orange, named their babies after players, and generally went crazy with support.

When the playoffs started against Pittsburgh, Miller's Broncos were ready to play. "We had the players ready and they played a hell of a game. We beat them, but I knew we had to get past the Raiders to really make our mark, and remember that they had won the Super Bowl the year before, so this was a good team."

But the Broncos had split the season series against the Raiders, winning in dominant fashion in Oakland prior to that defeat in Denver, so the Broncos felt deep down they could play against Oakland. Miller's theme for the week was: "Now we have them in our stadium for the title; don't waste this opportunity."

"Coming in here, I knew that this team had only two wins against Oakland in 14 years, and neither of those in Denver. That's not too good. I knew that they also had had some trouble on the road winning games. They weren't a bad team the year before I came here. They lacked cohesiveness and they lacked the fire and probably that's why you had the changes that led to my arrival. I came and I established that everybody is equal on the team. There's no one unit more important than any other regardless of what anybody thinks. We're all together in it."

Further, he had a special message for his team and the city regarding the Broncos' archrival Raiders.

"I said, 'I'll tell you what; we're going to beat the Oakland Raiders.' I said that in my first meeting and I said it many times in between. I took out a bunch of film. I had saved film through the years of the illegal hits of the Oakland players. We had won all of our first five games, and then we had our first meeting to rehash the previous game and get into the next one. I showed the team that little film I had put together. I kind of sensed that they were starting to catch on and say, 'Hey, this guy really does want to win this game. We are capable of doing this.' After all of the shooting was done and we had kicked the snot out of them in their park, after all that was done, now finally, we had beaten a good team on the road and had beaten Oakland. That was a message game. That meant to me that we had the right formula here and we're going to be OK."

THE GAME OF MY LIFE

The championship game was on New Year's Day, 1978, but quarterback Craig Morton did not feel in a partying mood. He had taken some hard hits on his right side in the Pittsburgh game. Red Miller's handling of the injury led the NFL to revise rules of how injuries are reported.

Morton was in the hospital all week. He did not watch film. He did not attend a team meeting. His right leg was black and blue from the ankle all the way up to his hip.

And the Broncos never told the press.

Miller got the game plan to his quarterback in the hospital, and they talked regularly, rehearsing it as well as possible considering the venue, but Miller answered the daily press questions by just saying Morton was doing well and would play on Sunday. Practice was closed, so there was no way to check. "I could never get away with that now," Miller accurately notes.

"Starting the next year, all injuries had to be reported a certain way. But at that time, I wasn't going to tell anybody."

All Miller and his staff could do was prepare Morton the best they could and hope their signal caller improved. "If a player told me that he couldn't play, he didn't play. I never said, 'You've got to play.'"

On Sunday in the locker room, Miller asked his passer how he felt about playing.

"Craig said, 'Well, Coach, I can't bend down to tie my shoes. If you tie my shoes, I'll go out and try it.' That's what he said. I went over to (reserve quarterback) Norris Weese and said, 'Get warmed up pretty good. You might be going in.' We went out there for pregame warm-ups and the first time Morton backed off center, I thought, 'Uh oh, this isn't going to work.' But I let him go and let him warm up. By the end, he was throwing real well. I said, 'What do you think, Craig?' He said, 'Well, Coach, I'll go as long as I can and if I wave to you, I'll come out.'"

The rookie head coach then met with his offensive linemen, and gave them the word, in no uncertain terms, that they had to protect their quarterback. "They did a hell of a job. He got hit once, but not very badly. The defense played super, and Morton played a hell of a game."

Morton threw two touchdown passes to Haven Moses, a 74-yarder in the first quarter and a 12-yard strike for the winning points with 7:17 left in the game. He completed 10 of 20 passes for 224 yards, the offensive line kept his uniform clean, and Morton never waved to Miller.

The Broncos had a balanced running game that produced 91 yards, running out the final 3:08 of the game, securing their most memorable and important win in franchise history to that date.

The fans stormed the field and tore the goal posts down. Unbridled revelry erupted throughout the city, and the Broncos would never be first-time champions again.

Fans had long said that it would be a miracle if the Broncos ever went to the Super Bowl, and when Miller watched with sage satisfaction as the team ran out the clock on the Raiders, legendary KOA radio play-by-play voice Bob Martin intoned, "The miracle has happened. The Denver Broncos are going to the Super Bowl."

"That single win turned the city around, in my opinion," Miller says. "That win told the NFL that we're here at the championship level, we belong here, and we're going to stay here, as contenders."

His words have proven prophetic, for the Broncos became a franchise that over a 30-year period would have more Super Bowl appearances than losing seasons.

AFTER THE CHEERING STOPPED

Following that magical championship season, Miller's Broncos finished 10-6 in 1978 and 1979. After an 8-8 record in 1980, a change in ownership occurred, and as frequently happens in those situations, the coach was out.

He went on to coach in the fledgling United States Football League for a couple of seasons and then embarked on another career, this time as a stockbroker.

He tackled it like he had everything else, became successful and enjoyed a 15-year run in the brokerage field before finally retiring for good.

"Just refer to that poem again. When someone told me I could not do something, I just buckled down that much harder to succeed, to prove I could.

"My wife, Nan, always says that I had to pound out the Xs and Os in my head before I could get the stock quotes in the paper, because I was always football. It was a hard beginning in that stock market. I went with Dean Witter. It was a hard beginning, but as I got on, the one thing I like to do is talk to people and meet people. I'm a people-guy so I kind of fit in."

He fit in for 15 years before his second retirement, but Red Miller has proven over the years that retirement from the business world just opens up a new career in life, one that now includes watching the development and accomplishments of his grandchildren, gardening in his Denver home, and spending lots of time with his beloved wife, Nan.

He remains active and popular in the Denver community, as well as being a regular attendee at all Broncos alumni functions.

Miller's hair may be gray, but he'll always be Red to Broncos fans.

And he will forever be the first coach to take the Denver Broncos to the Super Bowl.

Chapter 7

TOM JACKSON

BEFORE THE BRONCOS

The heart and soul of the Denver Broncos for 14 years, Tom Jackson was the emotional lynchpin of the franchise as it climbed out of the abyss of mediocrity to become a premier NFL team.

Always approachable by media and fans, Jackson stands at the top of the short list of most popular, most talkative, and most philosophical Broncos players.

Jackson begins, "I was born and raised in Cleveland, Ohio. I think my upbringing was fairly typical of a middle-class kid. I lived in the same house my entire youth. Everything was fairly typical until I was 13. My mom passed away. She had a stroke. She was really a healthy person and literally within a four-day period in 1965 she was gone."

Jackson was raised from that time through high school by his dad, forging a tremendous bond between the two.

"He kept me actively involved in sports. I played baseball, I wrestled, and I played football. I guess the intriguing thing to me about football—and I really didn't play organized ball 'til I was a sophomore in high school—was that I wasn't very good at it when I first started. I made the junior varsity team, but some kids were moved up to the varsity, and that was never me. I really didn't know what my future was going to be. I always thought that I was a better wrestler than I was a football player."

But by the time he got to the 11th grade he had improved significantly. "I started to realize that my quickness and my speed were what was going to separate me from the pack, and when I got to my senior year, I actually stood out."

He became captain of the team, a preview of what would come as a pro. "I played linebacker on defense, and the defense was structured around me as a rover back. Offensively, I played guard, which I think actually helped me later on to understand what was happening from the offensive side of the ball at least in terms of interior line."

Soon offers started to come in from colleges, but Jackson recalls, "I wasn't big. As I left high school at probably 195-200 pounds, I think a lot of colleges were kind of discouraged from giving me a scholarship, at least some of the bigger schools, because I didn't have the size. In fact one of the stories that I love to tell is that I wanted to go to Ohio State. That had been my dream, to go play for Woody Hayes."

But Jackson recalls how quickly that dream died. "One of his assistant coaches came to see me at John Adams High School. I was taken out of class to go talk to this assistant coach, who took me downstairs to my coach's office and sat me down. And when he saw me—and for my dad I think that this was one of those things that irked him 'til the day he died—the guy looked at me and said, 'I want to shoot straight with you. I think that you are too small to play linebacker in the Big Ten.' And I was crushed. I didn't let him know it at the time but I was crushed. I think it was kind of a motivating tool for me for the rest of my college career.

Against the Steelers on December 24, 1977, linebacker Tom Jackson's three turnovers—a fumble recovery and two interceptions—led to 17 of Denver's 34 points and the Broncos' first playoff win. *Rod Hanna/Denver Broncos*

"Enter Lee Corso, who came up from Louisville to see me. Corso was trying to rebuild the football program at Louisville. He was very honest with me, explaining that they were thinking about giving up their football program, which if you look at it today just seems crazy. But at the time, 1968-69, they were thinking about giving up football. I thought that his honesty was refreshing and took a visit."

Jackson earned a spot in the starting lineup as a sophomore and never again saw the bench while at Louisville, earning Missouri Valley Conference player of the year honors as a sophomore.

That really was a pivotal year. Even though he was still undersized he began to get the sense that there was a future beyond Louisville, a thought that received support from the cadre of scouts and pro personnel men who were beginning to sniff around the young linebacker. He played every game of his last three college seasons. "The durability factor was a big one in my favor. Even though I was undersized, I did manage to hold up, and at the time I was playing middle linebacker for Louisville."

He won championships (three) and player of the year honors (two), but one thing still gnawed at Jackson—and his father. "My dad used to always save me these articles, and one of them said that if I was two inches taller and 10 pounds heavier what a pro prospect I would be. I think I took that as a challenge, and yet the kind of overwhelming cockiness that many, many players have today in the game was just nonexistent in me. I still walked around with a sense that, 'Tom, you are going to really have to show your skills in order to make it in pro football.'"

THE SETTING

"When I got drafted by the Denver Broncos I really didn't know where Denver was. I had to go to a map."

But from the first moment of the first season, Jackson was in that class of players who lit up the practice field by play and attitude.

The team had never had a winning season in its history. "They never won, but I was surprised that we had so many of what I would

TOM JACKSON AT A GLANCE

POSITION: Linebacker
COLLEGE: University of Louisville
PLAYING HEIGHT, WEIGHT: 5-11, 220
YEARS PLAYED FOR BRONCOS: 1973-86
UNIFORM NUMBER: 57
NOTABLE: A 1992 inductee into the Denver Broncos Ring of Fame, Tom Jackson is one of only three Broncos to play 14 years with the team. He was named to the Pro Bowl three times (1977, 1978 and 1979), twice was named first team All-Pro (1977 and 1978), and was named by his teammates as Denver's most inspirational player for six consecutive seasons (1981~86). Jackson was inducted into the Colorado Sports Hall of Fame in 1989.
THE GAME: Pittsburgh at Denver, December 24, 1977

call quality players. It was obvious to me when I arrived. I knew it took a team to win, but we had some outstanding players on that team. We started to build, and we started to get some talent, adding to what was already there."

The Broncos had their first winning season in Jackson's rookie year, 1973, "Then all of a sudden we were ready to challenge, I thought, for playoffs and anything else that was out there. Our division was extremely tough because Oakland was in it. The Pittsburgh Steelers, who were a great football team, were in our conference. So it was pretty neat getting to the point where we could get to the playoffs, and in 1977 that was finally happening."

Jackson says that 1977 campaign remains seared in his memory bank. "I am going to mention one other game before I get to Pittsburgh. We played a game against the Baltimore Colts. When we played that game, we were both 9-1."

That contest is one in which Tom Jackson made the biggest play in Broncos history to that point, the play that would give the Broncos home-field advantage in the playoffs.

Jackson returned a Bert Jones interception 73 yards for the game's deciding score. "That play is the play that I have even played for my daughters to try to give them some sense of how enthusiastic Broncos fans were and everything else that happened to our team. We get to the playoffs, we have home field, and it's the Pittsburgh Steelers. In the 1970s it did not get any bigger than that."

THE GAME OF MY LIFE

The Pittsburgh Steelers were in the midst of winning four world titles in a six-year span when they came to Mile High Stadium for their divisional playoff game against the upstart Denver Broncos.

"Pick your poison," Jackson says. "Steelers. Raiders. You are going to have to play them and get by both of them in order to get yourself into the championship—into the Super Bowl. But the Steelers were first, and the first playoff opponent in Denver history. They had to come in to our place to play and I would be remiss if I didn't mention how tough it was for somebody to have to come into Mile High and win a game. My feeling was that if we had been on the road our task would have been a lot more difficult. But we were in Mile High and I was very confident that we would play well. I don't remember every play of the game, but it was a very physical football game. The ebb and flow of it was something that just sticks out in my mind."

Much of Jackson's emotional focus for the Broncos' first foray into the playoffs was once again on his father.

"My dad didn't travel a lot. He would see me if we played in Cleveland or he might come to Cincinnati but he wasn't going to come much further than that. My sister kind of followed me around a lot to see me play. So I told my dad, 'Look, it's the first game of the playoffs in Broncos history. I want you to come out to the game.' So he came to the game and I ended up having a pretty good game," Jackson says with great understatement.

Jackson ranged sideline to sideline for seven tackles against the Steelers, the high total for the Broncos' front seven, but two of the biggest plays of the game were two interceptions by Jackson. In addition to a fumble recovery play, three of Pittsburgh's drives ended with the ball in his hands.

The score was tied at 7-7 in the second period when Jackson recovered a fumble at the Pittsburgh 10-yard line, setting up Denver's go-ahead score. They went into the half tied at 14-14, but the Broncos never trailed in the game, and they led all the way in momentum, with their young linebacker exhorting the crowd.

Saving his most dramatic moments for the fourth quarter, Jackson stole two passes from Terry Bradshaw in the final period.

"It just felt to me—and I have always been proud of this—that game was the biggest game, at the time, that we had ever played, and I played my best in it. The interception that was really the most difficult one was right on the line of scrimmage, the first one.

"I backed up into the zone, but I was kind of reading one of the running backs that wasn't coming out. Terry Bradshaw gunned the ball, and I assumed it was either a square end or a curl that was right behind me. To this day I couldn't tell you because I never turned around, but I just jumped up and happened to hit the ball. It went straight up in the air and it came right down to me. But it was thrown so hard that I actually kind of thought that it could have gone anywhere. But it just came right down to me and I just weaved my way through a little bit of traffic. I got a pretty good return, and put our offense in pretty good position where they had a short field to work with."

It was a 32-yard return by Jackson and set up Jim Turner's second field goal in a 13-point fourth quarter for the Broncos.

"I was always hungry, trying to do more, and I remember that evening thinking, 'You had your hands on the ball three times and you never got to the end zone.'

"The other interception, the second one, was a little out-route late in the game where Terry throws to the flat. I got that one, then we walked off with a win and I think that our history really started to be written." That second interception came with the Broncos holding onto a 27-21 lead and Pittsburgh still believing it could win. Jackson returned it 17 yards to the Steelers 33, and two plays later Craig

Morton hit wide receiver Jack Dolbin on a 34-yard score to cement the win with 1:57 left to play.

Jackson's three turnovers had led to 17 of the Broncos' 34 points in the first-ever playoff win for the franchise.

"I think that for a long time people looked at the Denver Broncos and didn't really look at all. It was like we were stuck out in the mountains and they didn't give us the attention that they did to some of those east coast teams and some of the west coast teams, like the Raiders, the Chargers. Again, I think another thing that contributed was that for so many years we hadn't won. That game got us off to a good start in the playoffs—a good sense that if you had to come to Denver to play the Broncos you were likely going to be in trouble. It was a game in which we distinguished ourselves defensively, and for me I don't think I ever played a better game in a bigger game."

As big as his play was against the Steelers, his emotional leadership of the team and unrivaled bond with the Denver fans was just as huge a factor in the making of what the Broncos were becoming.

"Different people have different personalities. I kind of wore my emotions all of the time on my sleeve." Annually named the Broncos' most inspirational player by his teammates, Jackson says, "I think the reason that my teammates voted on me for that award—which I was so proud to have—was they knew that it was real. I wasn't trying to pump them up. I wasn't attempting to get the best out of them. I wasn't trying to encourage them at times that they were down. I wasn't just patting them on the back because they did well, I was doing it because I cared about them. I was doing it because it was just a natural part of me. Even when I was back in high school and in college I was the leader of my team. In fact, giving some of that leadership away was more difficult than people will ever know, and yet it was easy to do when the same types of people started to come to us. It was just a natural part of my game, and the emotion that I brought to the game was the same emotion that I have always brought to every other phase of my life."

The crowd was one with Jackson for his entire career, and the cheers for him as he left the field after beating the Steelers were deafening. He waved to the Broncos' sellout audience, and it seemed as if he was waving individually to every fan in attendance.

"I like the idea of the chemistry that comes from the concept of guys caring about each other. I believe wholeheartedly to this day that the teams that are the best, the teams that win the championship, are the teams that care about each other. That emotional part of me is something that was real, and I believe that I was perfectly suited to that football team, and to the development of the city and team as one.

"It never felt any better than that day against Pittsburgh. Winning for the first time is so special. I felt like I was perfectly suited to that group of guys, and I can really say this: That team that won that first playoff game, gave Denver that first thrill. I know that that team loved each other. There is no doubt in my mind that there was something present greater than just a bunch of football players playing a game. We were willing to sacrifice for each other and make it happen, and it was one of our proudest moments.

"I remember that drive home because I took that drive home with my dad.

"We had just won our first playoff game ever and my dad had been there for it, so he had gone with me all the way from watching me play high school ball and not being good enough to dress with the JV all the way to the excellence he saw that night during that game. I can tell you exactly what he said to me when we were driving home. My dad was very old school, so not a lot of accolades came out of my dad. As we are driving up to my house in Morrison he looked over at me and said, 'You know, you are a pretty good football player,' and nothing could have meant more to me. It almost brings tears to my eyes right now, but nothing greater in the world could have been said to me.

"It was just the best moment of my life."

AFTER THE CHEERING STOPPED

"When I retired, all the way from the house down to the complex I was totally in tears and bawling down the highway by myself. I was very composed by the time I got there; you know you don't want to be like this when you retire. You want to be able to thank people and tell them how much you appreciate what they have done for you and that includes assistant coaches and the media."

During the press conference, the media gave Jackson a rare gift, something unheard of—a standing ovation. They stood up and applauded Tom Jackson, TJ, not because he was a great player. They applauded him because of his relationship with them as a stand-up guy.

After retirement, Jackson moved to Cincinnati, partly to be near his father. His dad died in 1995. But his father's influence was very much a factor as Jackson's post-football career began to unfold.

"The media and I had an extraordinary relationship. I was never afraid to talk to them about what I felt, and I think they always knew they were going to get the truth out of me and from me. Anyway, I retired, and within weeks I got a call from NBC in New York. They flew me in for an audition and took me into the next room after the audition and they were going to hire me on the spot. I told them—and this really came from my dad, that if you have a huge decision to make, try to take a week to think about it—so I asked them if I could have a week to think about it. During that week ESPN called and I went in and did the audition there as well and met Chris Berman. I really can't tell anybody exactly what happened except some of that same type of chemistry that exists in football exists between Chris and me.

"So I joined ESPN. From that moment to this, I have two Emmys sitting in front of me right now in my office. I have an ACE award sitting somewhere in here that my wife has put up. We have *Monday Night Football*. We have one of the highest-rated shows in the history of the NFL and in prime time. I had a chance to stay in the business of football and I can't tell you how lucky and blessed I feel in my life for what has happened to me. I feel like somebody has watched over me my entire life. I have got a great family—my wife, Jennifer, and two lovely daughters, Morgan and Taylor.

"What I do is the most fun that you can have other than playing the game. I always tell my wife and friends that if I could choose the two things that I would love to do in life it would be to play pro football, which I did and was able to play for 14 years, and to talk about football and have fun and be on TV and I have been doing that now for two decades."

The end of his career did not mark the last time Jackson was ever on the Denver sideline for a big game, literally or figuratively.

"Being inducted into the Denver Broncos Ring of Fame is the greatest honor that has ever been given to me. That moment where you get a chance to thank those fans for what they meant to you, to get the chance to kind of soak in everything at Mile High Stadium that one last time, there is nothing quite like that. I have gotten a lot of awards within the context of playing football and doing TV, but the best moment for me that has to do with the Denver Broncos was the moment that that pass got knocked down and they won the championship of the world in Super Bowl XXXII.

"I had been invited to be in the locker room before the game, so I was there. I was on the sideline when they played Green Bay, but I had to leave because the ESPN set for postgame and for everything that we were going to do was back at our hotel. So I had to leave near the beginning of the third quarter. TD (Terrell Davis) had come out of the locker room and I knew that he had had that headache, or migraine. He had come out, and I think the first thing he did was fumble the ball. So I left and got back to the hotel walking to our set, which literally is on one of the waterways so we could have water in the background—a beautiful scenic shot. I stopped, and at first I thought, 'It isn't right to do this, but I am going to do it anyway.' I stopped and I prayed and asked God to please give them this. They had played their way back into the game and we had gone through all of those losses in the Super Bowl. When they won that game, the moment that that game ended—I will tell you exactly where I was. I was in a room with Sterling Sharpe. Sterling and I got up and hugged like it was nobody's business. Sterling, because of his brother Shannon, and me because I was a former Bronco."

To the Broncos franchise, Tom Jackson will never be a "former" Bronco.

Chapter 8

CHARLEY JOHNSON

BEFORE THE BRONCOS

Charley Johnson is one of pro football's Renaissance men—player, army veteran, doctor, professor. How many NFL quarterbacks hold doctoral degrees? Johnson was and is on the short list in that regard.

He came to the Broncos as an already-grizzled NFL vet, after previous stints with the St. Louis Cardinals and Houston Oilers, where he had established himself as a winner who could sling the football.

"I got to start in my second year in St. Louis," Johnson notes. "And in my very first start we tied Washington, and we threw the ball quite a bit. I broke a lot of Paul Christman's records, which were long-standing with the Cardinals. In my third year, we missed out on the division championship by half a game, but I threw 28 touchdown passes, which was the second most anybody had thrown in a season at that time."

Johnson was rewarded, as quarterbacks always are, with a trip to the Pro Bowl.

Johnson's Cards barely missed the playoffs in 1964 and 1965, but Johnson was demonstrating an electric ability to move the ball downfield. "We played Cleveland at Cleveland in the second game of the '65 season, and I threw six touchdown passes against them, which for our team pretty much showed us that we could be competitive with the NFL champions. And not only that, but beat them on their home turf, and beat them badly."

Meanwhile, football was just part of his equation: Johnson was doing triple duty as quarterback, army officer, and graduate student.

"I was in St. Louis nine years all together, got hurt later in '65, and in '66 we changed coaches. I got hurt again, and then in '67 I had to go on active duty. I had been an ROTC graduate, so I was a commissioned officer. And I was going to graduate school to keep from going to active duty. But I was juggling a lot, and when I was having surgery, I did not sign up for enough courses, and they called me in immediately."

Astonishingly, Johnson did not miss a season, despite being on active duty. "The Cardinals were great about keeping me on the roster," he remembers, "and I commuted from wherever I was. The army assigned me to NASA, and I worked at NASA for almost two years, and I commuted to the games from there. I definitely flew a lot, and played in a lot of games. I never missed a game in the two years."

Why graduate school in addition to everything else on his plate? Simple, says Johnson. "I think at that time quite a few of us were very much aware that football was not going to be a lifetime career, and we had other interests and other obligations, of some kind, to either family, or our parents, to do the best we could and continue our educations as far as we could."

Ultimately, Johnson would earn a master's degree from Washington University in St. Louis in 1971 and a doctoral degree in chemical engineering from his alma mater, New Mexico State

---

Already a veteran when he joined the Broncos in 1972, quarterback Charley Johnson piloted the team to its first winning season the next year. *Courtesy of the Denver Broncos*

University. Johnson and Frank Ryan of the Cleveland Browns, who played in the same era, are the only quarterbacks in memory who share the remarkable distinction of earning doctoral degrees while slinging the ball at a high level in the NFL.

Johnson played for the Houston Oilers in 1970 and '71, but the experience was short-lived for a variety of reasons. "I got hurt again early in 1970 when we were 3-1. Head coach Wally Lemm retired mid-season. Then they drafted Dan Pastorini and Lynn Dickey, and after 1971 they decided to keep the two younger guys and traded me to Denver."

And according to Johnson, "That was like going from the outhouse to the penthouse in one step."

THE SETTING

Now Charley Johnson is a member of the Denver Broncos Ring of Fame—an honored alum of one of pro football's storied franchises. But it wasn't that way when he arrived in the Mile High City.

Fellow Ring of Famer and teammate Haven Moses has the one great, definitive quote about Charley Johnson: "He taught us how to win."

But it was a lesson learned the hard way.

Bluntly put, the Broncos were bad, a franchise that had never had a winning season in over a decade of play, and a team not on the national radar in any way. The Broncos were a nonentity in pro football.

Still, Johnson was happy for a change of scenery—any change of scenery—and his New Mexico background gave him familiarity with the region populated by his new team. While diplomatic about his experience with the Oilers, he says, "I had been in Houston for two seasons, and I had three head coaches and five surgeries, so that pretty well explains my feelings at the time.

"Even then, despite the record of the team, the fans in Denver were terrific. They were excited about the Broncos, and I could see right away that they had the makings of a good team."

CHARLEY JOHNSON AT A GLANCE

POSITION: Quarterback
COLLEGE: New Mexico State University
PLAYING HEIGHT, WEIGHT: 6-1, 200
YEARS PLAYED FOR BRONCOS: 1972-75
UNIFORM NUMBER: 12
NOTABLE: Inducted into the Denver Broncos Ring of Fame in 1986, Charley Johnson quarterbacked the Broncos to their first winning season (7-5-2 in 1973), a landmark moment in franchise history. He made the All-AFC team (as picked by UPI and Pro Football Weekly) after the 1973 season.
THE GAME: Denver at Oakland, October 22, 1972

Under the surface, there were elements on which a team could be built. Floyd Little was a fantastic player, and they had a brand new head coach in the always enthusiastic John Ralston. "Ralston was an extremely good motivator and organizer in every aspect of play and organization, so I felt very fortunate to step in there and maybe make a contribution," Johnson recalls.

Quarterback Steve Ramsey was having the problems that most young quarterbacks have getting rid of the ball. "He was not expecting his offensive line to do its job all the time. I had had that situation before, and when I got a chance to play, I told 'em, 'I don't care if you block anybody, they're not going to get me. I'm going to turn loose of the ball. You receivers better be ready.' So that was good to hear for everybody, and we didn't have any more sacks, and we were able to move the football."

Indeed, the entire team's response to a veteran quarterback who had been through the NFL wars was warm and welcoming, marking a subtle turning point in franchise history. Johnson notes, "The more they found out about me, the more they could see that it was real, and as I played more and more, they realized that I had been there. I knew the stage at which they were standing as far as progressing as a team, and gosh, they all bought into it. They all bought into it."

Buying into it was one thing for a young Denver club that had never won before, but there was still a notorious division rival—the Oakland Raiders.

THE GAME OF MY LIFE

The Oakland Raiders were a great team, and their games against the Broncos were absolute disasters for the team in orange. From 1963 through 1971 the two teams had played 18 times, and Denver had an inauspicious 0-17-1 record in those contests.

It has been suggested that the 23-23 Denver-Oakland tie in 1973 was Johnson's greatest game, but, with the perspective and analysis of a true leader, Johnson quickly shot down that theory.

"In 1973, the Broncos had their first winning season, and that tie was a great game, but the stage for it was set one year earlier. In 1972, we went out to play the Raiders, and that was the first time they had ever seen me. I had never played against Oakland before, and Big John (Madden), the coach, was kind of surprised by what we did."

On October 22, 1972 the Broncos announced to the Raiders and the NFL that they were on their way to removing the "doormat" tag from the franchise name.

The Broncos beat the Raiders by a score of 30-23 in Oakland, actually going ahead by a 24-3 margin before the Raiders were able to claw their way back into the game. Along the way, Johnson completed 20 of 28 passes for 361 yards and two touchdowns.

"That was quite a surprise for the Raiders," Johnson understates. "We had worked out a way for our receivers to battle against their bump-and-run cornerbacks, who had been very, very successful against our receivers and those around the league before, and continued to be after that. But we figured out a way for our receivers to look back, and not put their hands up until the last second, and I was throwing the ball just over the defensive back's head and shoulders. We called it 'over the shoulder.' Jerry Simmons had a marvelous day, Floyd Little fooled 'em and threw a touchdown pass himself, and it was just one of those great days."

Johnson's first TD strike was a 21-yarder to tight end Billy Masters in the first quarter, his second to the brilliant Little on a 37-yard pass. Then, Little's halfback pass to Jerry Simmons shocked the Raiders for a 35-yard second-period score. That made it 21-3, and the Broncos never looked back. Their decade of ugliness against Oakland, marked by that 0-17-1 mark, was about to end, and the new world was in sight.

Johnson's memories are vivid, and he led the Broncos in ways other than just by passing the ball. "I threw for a first down one time, and I went down in front of their bench at about the 30-yard-line, and Big John came down to me and yelled, 'What do you think you're doing, bleep, bleep, bleep, bleep, bleep.' And I called the referee over and told him, 'Would you get that big fat guy down there back in his bench area where he belongs?'

"It was such fun, not just having success, but having success in an arena that was notorious for beating up on the Broncos when they came to town. We had a tremendous game plan put together by (offensive coordinator) Max Coley, who was not familiar to the Raiders either."

Coley had come to Denver from Pittsburgh in the NFC. "He was able to prepare us to do some things that the Raiders had not seen, but that fit our personnel," Johnson adds.

"The way we matched up with them that day was very, very good. This game was very significant because it set the stage for the team becoming a winner."

Ralston had already made a key trade for Haven Moses, was starting to add players through the draft, and according to the quarterback, "The guys we already had were developing and getting confidence. We became a very, very strong team, and proved it in 1973 and 1974.

"That game was certainly in the top five of my entire 15-year career, with every team, statistically for me; but because of its impact on our growth as a team, it was enormous for me."

And enormous for the Broncos as well. The next year, Johnson's leadership helped lead Denver to its first winning season, and began to establish the franchise in the NFL hierarchy.

AFTER THE CHEERING STOPPED

Johnson continued to have professional growth and success in the years following his pro playing days, and he acknowledges that being a star quarterback did not hurt the development of his post-football career.

"Certainly, the fame, celebrity, and financial 'goodies' from playing ball helped me in my engineering career. I lived in Houston for 30 years, and half of that time I had my own business.

"I would have to say it was not difficult, being a sales engineer like I was, to get in and see the important people in the different companies. Football gave us something to talk about, and in the southwest, the oil patch and football kind of go hand in hand."

Johnson followed up his success as a sales engineer with a return to academia at his alma mater in Las Cruces, New Mexico, where he is a professor in chemical engineering. In his spare time, he still serves part-time as an assistant to the New Mexico State University president in matters of athletic progress.

The final footnote to his Broncos career was not written until 1986, when owner Pat Bowlen called Charley Johnson and informed him that he had been selected to the Denver Broncos Ring of Fame.

"I was terribly surprised by that," says Johnson. "When Pat Bowlen called me, I realized, 'Wow! That was significant.' My father died two weeks before I was inducted, so I was able to eulogize him at the ceremony, and that was a wonderful moment for me."

Before his arrival in Denver, the Broncos had never won.

Since then, they have almost never lost. In the more than three decades since the arrival of Charley Johnson, they've had only five losing seasons.

Chapter 9

RICH KARLIS

BEFORE THE BRONCOS

You always remember a barefoot kicker. But if that's all anyone remembers about Rich Karlis, they are missing a lot of information about Karlis as a player, a teammate, and as a community activist.

He kicked barefoot for the Broncos, but as in every story, things did not begin the way they ended.

He grew up loving to punt the football, but did not kick much from a tee or a hold. Karlis remembers that he played a lot of kickball in the playground growing up, and learned to kick a football as well. "I kicked it 'sideways,' I guess, as opposed to 'soccer-style,' since I never played soccer in my life. That was just something I loved to do in the backyard, hitting the wires over the house, or landing it on the hood of a car, then getting yelled at, things like that."

"My football dream kind of faded a little bit in high school. I didn't grow as fast as some kids, and I always wanted to be a wide receiver or defensive back, and just didn't have the size of it early." Nevertheless, on a whim he went out for football as a high school senior, and quickly discovered coaches wanted him to focus more on punting and kicking than playing a position from scrimmage.

Karlis acknowledges that he had a pretty decent season, although the team only won one game. "But it kind of lit a spark in me, and I felt that I would like to keep getting better at it, keep doing it."

His next stop was as a walk-on at the University of Cincinnati, where they kept him as a punter. He remembers that as a walk-on, he didn't get a decal on his helmet until the last game of the season. But then, the spring of his freshman year in college, they switched him from punting to just kicking.

And he was about to make a major change in his style.

"At that point, I had seen Tony Franklin kicking barefoot at Texas A&M, and I was intrigued by how he kicked the ball," Karlis recalls. "But I figured I better learn in a hurry if I wanted a chance to play. So I started messing around with kicking barefoot, initially kicking off a two-inch tee, but quickly went to a one-inch tee. I spent a lot of time in the summers trying to hone that craft."

By his sophomore year he was kicking off for the varsity, and they finally put him on scholarship after his junior year. When his career with the Bearcats ended, he found someone to represent him and got a tryout with the Houston Oilers in 1981. That "three-week cup of coffee" was most memorable for a little seed of encouragement planted by Oilers player personnel director Mike Holovak. "I think you're good enough, don't give this up yet," Holovak encouraged, as he had a hundred times before to guys who lacked just that little bit.

But Karlis took the encouraging words to heart, went back to school to finish his degree in economics, and wrote letters to every team in the NFL. The Broncos were one of those teams that got one of those letters, and they sent a reply. "It was one of those nice form letters, saying they had a tryout camp on May 8, 1982. I thought it

---

Rich Karlis kicked for the Broncos for nine years and was the last NFL kicker to employ the barefoot technique.
Courtesy of the Denver Broncos

was an invitation-only camp until I showed up and realized it was an open invitation," Karlis says.

Yes, open to everyone.

The scene most closely resembled the *Star Wars* bar on a football field—the most bizarre and outlandish 478-man collection of wannabe players (and in almost every case, never-would-be) imaginable.

Among the 478 in attendance were a lot of kickers—enough that it took a couple of hours just to attempt two kicks each from 20, 30, 40, and 50 yards. Coaches, scouts, press, and other observers were chuckling to themselves, and sometimes not just to themselves.

"I remember having a tremendous amount of doubt. Could I distance myself from everyone else to even be looked at? I remember saying a little prayer, about not giving up on myself at this point. I had trained so hard in the winter at the U of C—lifting, running, stairs. I had to mentally work my way past the point of looking at the surreal environment of a camp like that—my shirt had number 192 on it. I kept reminding myself of how hard I had worked, and that I had earned the right to be there; so I went out and gave it my best."

Karlis went out and kicked extremely well. Broncos executive John Beake tried to sign him that day, but the jobless young kicker held out for a signing bonus of $500. "So I could pay for my airfare! That was a big win for me!"

THE SETTING

Having made the team and established himself as an NFL kicker, Karlis had a fine season in 1986 for a Denver Broncos franchise that was attempting to return to the Super Bowl for the first time since 1977.

But it would not be easy. The Broncos had won the AFC Western Division and beaten the New England Patriots in the divisional round game, setting up a trip to Cleveland, where the Browns and their notorious "Dawg Pound" fans were waiting with the best record in the AFC.

RICH KARLIS AT A GLANCE

POSITION: Kicker
COLLEGE: University of Cincinnati
PLAYING HEIGHT, WEIGHT: 6-0, 180
YEARS PLAYED FOR BRONCOS: 1982-1 988
UNIFORM NUMBER: 3
NOTBALE: Rich Karlis is third in Denver Broncos history in points scored (655), field goals made (137), field goal percentage (.710) and extra points made (244). His streak of 13 consecutive field goals made (during the 1984-85 seasons) is second best in franchise history. Karlis was named to the Football Digest All-Rookie team in 1982, and connected on the first 11 field-goal attempts of his Broncos career.
THE GAME: Denver at Cleveland, January 11, 1987

The visiting locker room in the antiquated Cleveland Stadium was famously inadequate, and Karlis sat on the concrete floor outside that locker room, just staring into space before the pregame warm-ups.

Elaborating, Karlis adds, "We had played so many close games throughout the year. When I think of that game, I don't think of it as being in color, I almost remember it as being in black and white, like it was kind of a throwback to that Giants-Colts game back in 1958. It was so blustery; there was not really any grass on the field. The dirt was painted green. It was an old, rickety stadium that had outlived its time. The locker rooms were so small—not designed for the larger roster sizes of 47 players. I was just trying to find someplace where I could go and concentrate and get my mind focused."

Among his pregame thoughts were some that included the Cleveland organization. "The Browns had expressed no interest in me when I was going for tryouts, basically telling me, 'We don't think you have the talent to play.'"

The young kicker's family had driven up from Salem, Ohio, for the game on that cold January 11, and they were among the pronounced minority in a vocal crowd that added to the "throwback" feeling of the day.

The Browns fans were nothing if not passionate, and being vocal during the game itself was just part of their contribution to the game. "Knowing how passionate those Browns fans were—given the fact that they had driven around our hotel for two straight nights (the Broncos had arrived in Cleveland Friday as per NFL requirements), honking their horns, so we couldn't get to sleep—we knew we would be in an intimidating atmosphere, that's for sure."

THE GAME OF MY LIFE

The atmosphere was contentious, and Karlis remembers it well. "Just going out for pregame warm-ups, the crowd was already pretty whipped up. We kicked at the closed end of the field first for warm-ups, and there was a lot of space behind those posts. Then coming down together where the Dawg Pound was—right on the back of the end zone—there were dog bones littered all over the field. We barely kicked (10 or 12 kicks) at that end, because it was so hostile down there." The fans were making their presence known, as they would all afternoon.

The game itself is enshrined in Broncos and NFL lore as "The Drive"—the game when John Elway came of age in his Hall of Fame career. It was a defensive struggle, bitterly contested on the painted dirt of Cleveland Stadium.

Karlis kicked a field goal in the second quarter that led to a 10-10 score at halftime, and added one in the third as the only score of the period. "I don't remember anything special about the first two field goals. It was a defensive struggle the whole game, and the kicks were routine, but every kick mattered in a game like that."

Neither team was generating a lot of offense in a back-and-forth game in which each defense forced six punts. As the fourth quarter began, Karlis' field goals of 19 and 26 yards had accounted for half of Denver's point total, but Karlis recalls that Cleveland's veteran kicker Mark Moseley was having a fine day as well.

"He gave us a tough time on kickoffs all day. We wrestled a lot with Moseley's kickoffs, as he kind of knuckleballed it down to you."

The Browns took the lead with just over five minutes remaining in regulation, and Moseley kicked off to the Broncos again. Denver fell on Moseley's bouncer at the two-yard line, and it was first and 98 for the Broncos' Super Bowl chances.

Elway engineered one of the greatest drives in NFL history—98 yards on 15 plays, culminating with a five-yard strike to wide receiver Mark Jackson, setting Karlis up to tie the game with a half minute left.

"The kick that actually stands out in my mind the most was that extra point, after Elway threw the TD to Jackson. It was at the Dawg Pound end. Things were flying everywhere, and the thought flashed through my head, that 'this would be a really bad time to miss a kick.' Especially down at that end, where the field was just littered with dog bones."

Karlis routinely made the kick to tie the score in what has been called one of the NFL's greatest games ever. "I remember after making the extra point, (Cleveland defensive back) Frank Minnifield landed at my legs. I went to help him up and he kind of pushed me away. Tom Jackson jumped in and was all over the situation—as TJ always was— and I just remember thinking of how much frustration they were dealing with on the defensive side, having just given up a 98-yard touchdown drive to tie the game."

The tension was reaching palpable levels on both sides. On the kickoff following the extra point, Karlis nearly blew it. "I actually kicked it out of bounds. You can imagine looking over and seeing Dan (Reeves), and his head ready to blow off his shoulders. But in those days you just got a five-yard penalty and kicked again, and I hit a great kickoff. We tackled them inside the 20."

Cleveland ran out the clock, setting up overtime. The Browns took the opening kickoff but were forced to punt after being unable to move the ball. Elway took over at the Denver 25 and started the final drive of the day.

"Once we got past our 40-yard line, given the weather and conditions, I thought we would be fairly conservative. I started warming up when we crossed the 50. I had to pull the net almost onto the field to warm up, because the sidelines were nothing but snow and ice and dirt. I started trying to get my focus and be ready."

While Karlis was getting his foot and mind right, Elway was driving the Broncos. A 22-yard pass to tight end Orson Mobley put the ball on the Cleveland 48, and after a short running play and an incomplete pass, Elway connected with wide receiver Steve Watson for 28 yards. It was first down at the Cleveland 22, and from there the Broncos safely handed the ball to running back Sammy Winder, who notched gains of five, two, and one yard. On third down at the Cleveland 15, Karlis trotted onto the field for what would be a 33-yard field-goal attempt.

"I ran out onto the field, and was trying to find a decent place to kick out of, which there wasn't. I kicked some dirt away, and all that did was make a hole. So I then pushed it all back and tried to stomp it down. Of course, (holder Gary) Kubiak was as cool as a cucumber. He walked over and said, 'Hey, after you make this kick I'm going to jump into your arms.' And I remember thinking, 'What the heck is he thinking?' He's already got me making the kick! But it made me chuckle. When I ran out onto the field, John was so charged up—just as wired as wired can be—yelling at me, 'It's just like practice, just like practice.' And that just shows how tough that kick was for John, because he would rather have it on his shoulders than anyone else's.

"My biggest fear was my plant foot, because it was just like a sand trap out there. And sure enough, I planted into that kick, and my left foot continued to slide, which put me a little closer to the ball than I would desire. Historically, I never put a hook on my ball; they were all pretty true, whether I made them or missed them. That ball left my foot, and the place just went quiet, and waited. When it went over the post, I looked straight down the post at the referee. He took two steps forward and put his arms up, without any hesitation. I turned back and looked for Kubiak, but he was sprinting to the sidelines in jubilation. But here was (linebacker) Rick Dennison running right at me. I jumped in his arms, he landed on top of me, and it became a pile of people, under which I could not breathe!"

The scene was incredible, stunning in its silence. There were so few Broncos fans in attendance that it was possible to pick them out by their voices throughout the stadium. They were the only ones cheering. Rich Karlis had transformed the crowd of 79,973 into attendees at a wake.

His memories are all great ones. "I tell people my life is so charmed. If you would have asked me about this my senior year of high school, I would not have thought of that. To have a chance to play, and to have a chance to play in Denver, and then have a chance to play in such big games, before great fans—it is so surreal.

"And as an athlete, you never know when you are going to get that tap on the shoulder. It was great to have the chance at that kind of career-defining moment, and you hope you're up for it. You never know when it's going to happen, or if that moment will happen at all, and you hope you are ready for it."

AFTER THE CHEERING STOPPED

Karlis had the good fortune to travel to a lot of cities, but was drawn back to Denver and its quality of life and daily sunshine.

Once in retirement, Karlis put that second shoe on and jumped into things with both feet. "The best advice my attorney, Ron Grinker, gave me was to take the free time that you have, and maximize the opportunity the Broncos have given you, by doing something positive in the community. I wanted to have an opportunity to make a difference in people's lives."

Karlis took the lessons his parents taught him and the community work that he was encouraged to do, and translated it all into Family Tree, an organization that provides guidance, counsel, and shelter to victims of domestic violence. "Those are some of the most meaningful things I have ever done. I put my heart and soul into Family Tree, and to this day, people come up to me and mention my Points for People program."

He kept his Points for People program going for 20 years, and Family Tree is still being supported. Karlis makes no secret of the importance these programs have had in his life.

After dabbling with various sports marketing programs in retirement, he moved over to Qwest as the new century got underway. Karlis embraced the new communications challenges in a big way.

As director of corporate sponsorships and events for Qwest Communications, he is at the forefront of new sponsorship promotions for his firm, which included work on the details involved for the new Seattle Seahawks stadium, Qwest Field.

"I'm still kicking, but now I keep both shoes on," says Karlis.

Chapter 10

BILLY THOMPSON

BEFORE THE BRONCOS

Billy Thompson was a longtime team captain for the Denver Broncos and had 61 forced turnovers in a glittering pro career. Not many players are as well known by their initials as by their names, but "BT" rapidly elevated himself to that position with the Broncos.

However, before he was BT, he was growing up in Greenville, South Carolina, and spending his summers in Chicago with an uncle and aunt. "My mother had two sisters in Chicago, so my brother, sister, and I used to spend summer vacations in Chicago," he says, adding that it was his uncle who sent him in the direction of a local Boys and Girls Club. "I went down to the club and they talked about playing baseball and asked if I would like to play, I said sure, and that was actually how I won my first trophy in sports."

It was in 1957, and young Billy's team won the City League Little League Baseball Championship in Chicago with the Boys and Girls Club when he was still a pre-teen. "It was really a big thrill for me, but I couldn't stay for the ceremonies because I had to get back to South

Carolina because the summer was over, so they mailed me all of my stuff."

He said he still has that trophy from 1957, but had no idea at the time how much of a harbinger it would be of his future career.

He went on to a great college career at Maryland State (now University of Maryland Eastern Shore), where Thompson excelled as a defensive back in football and outfielder in baseball. It was not a large school, but then as now, you can't hide talent, and the gifted young athlete was drafted in two sports—by the American Football League's Broncos in the third round and by the Major League Baseball Baltimore Orioles.

Thompson knew he had natural talent, something that was reinforced by every football scout who saw him, and he was not too interested in spending several years in the minor leagues.

He was on his way to Denver.

THE SETTING

To properly set the stage for the championship game that is Thompson's game of his life, one must take note of the situation he came into when drafted by the Broncos. The franchise was just starting to find its way in pro football when he came aboard, and he was leading the way before his 1969 rookie season was over.

For his first five years he played corner with skill and an enthusiasm that was new to the Broncos' defense. "I was excited, no doubt about it, and coming to a team that had not had a lot of success, I was really chomping at the bit to try and help the team win."

He made his presence felt immediately, setting a pro football record as a rookie that still stands, becoming the only player in the history of the game to lead the league in both kickoff returns and punt

Drafted by the Broncos and the baseball Baltimore Orioles in 1969, safety Billy Thompson chose football and went on to a glowing 13-year career in Denver.
Courtesy of the Denver Broncos

returns in the same season. He was off to a great start, but the team was still a chronic loser.

This would change, with Thompson at the forefront, but he volunteers that there was plenty of help along the way to becoming the leader in Denver's defensive backfield. "I was really molded by one of the coaches, Joe Collier. He called me into his office and told me after my fifth year they were going to move me to safety, and I really wasn't that excited about it because I really wanted to play at corner. He said to me, 'Billy, I really want to explain something to you. You would be more valuable to us playing safety. The way that this defense is going to be run you are going to be a key player in it. You need to make that adjustment, and I am going to help you make that adjustment because you are going to have to learn the game a lot more.'"

So the new safety spent that entire summer with Collier watching film three days a week, talking with the defensive coordinator and understanding what his role would be. Thompson notes, "That particular summer making the change from corner to safety was very critical in my career as far as really learning and understanding what defenses were doing. And from that point on I think that I became a student of the game and got really involved and became proud of myself for not making mistakes. I ended up wanting to be the best at that position that I could possibly be. I knew to do that I would really need to study a lot and I did. I really started to study the game and understand football. It made me a much better player, especially later in my career when the speed went down a bit but the knowledge went up. I could make up for my speed by making sure I was in the right position. Joe Collier was really responsible for that."

Thompson learned fast, and no lesson ever had to be taught twice. Talented enough to be a cornerback, he ultimately took his leadership skills and settled in at safety, where he guided the Broncos' defensive backfield to that image-changing win over the Raiders.

Thompson displayed a unique blend of ability and leadership skills, highlighted by 61 career forced turnovers and so many big plays, including another record that still stands.

No one in pro football history has returned more fumbles for touchdowns than the four by Thompson.

BILLY THOMPSON AT A GLANCE

POSITION: Safety
COLLEGE: Maryland State College (now University of Maryland Eastern Shore)
PLAYING HEIGHT, WEIGHT: 6-1, 201
YEARS PLAYED FOR BRONCOS: 1969-1981
UNIFORM NUMBER: 36
NOTABLE: A 1987 inductee into the Denver Broncos Ring of Fame, Billy Thompson was the first player to play 13 seasons for the Broncos, and was team captain for many years. Thompson still ranks second on the Broncos' all-time list for games started with 178, first in consecutive starts with 156, and eighth in games played with 179. He finished his career with 61 forced turnovers (most in team history), 40 of which came via interceptions (third in team history). Thompson holds two NFL records, one of which has stood for more than three decades. In 1969, he became the only player in pro football history to lead the league in both kick-off returns and punt returns in the same season, and he is also one of only two players ever to return four opponent fumbles for touchdowns. Thompson was a three-time Pro Bowl selection (1977, 1978, and 1981) and earned All-NFL honors twice (1977 and 1978) and All-AFC honors four times (1977-79, 1981). He was inducted into the Colorado Sports Hall of Fame in 1985.
THE GAME: Oakland at Denver, January 1, 1978

But individual success is trumped by team failure, and the Broncos' history was gnawing at Thompson, the team, and its fandom.

It was 1977, Thompson had been a star for the Broncos since 1969, and they had not won anything.

"It is not hard for me to pick the game that matters most to me. The top teams in the AFC West were Oakland and the Chiefs, both teams dominating in the early years, the '70s and early '80s. Early on, we hadn't had that much success against them and that just ate at us."

But the AFC title game in 1977 really and truly turned the tide for the organization. "People started to believe that we could be competitive with the two marquee teams. After we played them for the right to go to the Super Bowl it made everybody aware that the Broncos were now a team that had to be dealt with in the AFC West. Since that time we have been one of the top teams in the AFC West. So that's how big the game was."

Had the Broncos lost that year it would've just been another season when the Raiders brushed them off on their way to the Super Bowl. The Raiders had been pushing the Broncos around for more than a decade. The Broncos had just two wins and two ties against Oakland in 28 games between the teams from 1963-1976.

In all the seasons the Broncos have ever played, perhaps none has been as magical as 1977. It was the first time they had won, and as with many things in life, there is nothing that compares with the first of anything. Red Miller had taken over as head coach, and there was a new enthusiasm in the air.

According to Thompson, "I thought we had the team to really do something. It was a special year. We were picked to finish somewhere near the bottom of the AFC West, and I liked that because we came in under the radar."

The Broncos started off 6-0 and never looked back. They lost their first game to the Raiders at Mile High Stadium on October 16, 1977, in a game that suggested to outsiders that it was still business as usual in the AFC West, with Oakland getting the wins that made the difference. "But we had some great games throughout the year—home, road, ahead, coming from behind. It was just different. We won the close games that we always used to lose, and there was no doubt in my mind that we were destined to be a great team that year."

So the Broncos finished 12-2, won their division, and secured home-field advantage for the playoffs. They beat Pittsburgh in the first postseason game in franchise history. And that win set up another game against the Raiders, the ultimate villains for Broncos fans.

The Raiders had already won in Denver once in 1977, and they came back to Mile High with confidence after an overtime playoff win at Baltimore against the Colts. But then, the Raiders were always confident when they played the Broncos.

However, this was truly the start of a new era in Denver—it was just that no one knew it yet. "One of the reasons why I was so excited about playing the Raiders was because Art Shell and I had been college teammates for three years. We were very close and he told me that when he was drafted by the Raiders he told them about me and the Raiders had been trying to get me ever since. Al Davis said that one of the biggest mistakes he ever made was not drafting me. I had personal motivation, and there was really only one team that was the one for us to beat to win a championship. It just had to be the Raiders."

That's the way the fans felt as well. It just had to be the Raiders. The fans who had supported the team for so many years would have this game at home for the right to go to the Super Bowl.

THE GAME OF MY LIFE

This was not only the game of Billy Thompson's life, it was the game of the Broncos' life as a franchise. Pro football's poster child for losing teams had a chance to go to the Super Bowl, but Denver would have to defeat one of the storied teams of the era to make that dream a reality.

The box score for that championship game shows Thompson with five tackles, tied for second most on the team that day. But the stats do not show big hits, leadership, intimidation, or will.

Denver's Orange Crush defense held the Raiders under 300 yards and limited Oakland's potent offense to just 17 points in a grim physical battle which Denver won, 20-17. But the score just shows numbers, not the unlimited emotional response of a city, a state— indeed, a time zone—for such a win.

"We knew it was going to be a hard-hitting kind of game," the captain remembers.

The Raiders were the defending world champions and came to Denver with a vast array of offensive weapons. "Our key for that game was to make sure that we didn't give up big plays, and we didn't.

"All game long the ebb and flow, from a defensive standpoint, was one in which we felt comfortable that they couldn't move the ball on us for any long periods of time. We had to stay patient because they were a big play kind of team."

The Broncos had to make sure they managed to keep that vaunted Oakland offense in some type of check, and that meant containing the likes of Ken Stabler at quarterback, Fred Biletnikoff at wide receiver, and Dave Casper at tight end. Holding them down was a huge key to the game for Denver, and a great burden for the defense throughout the day.

Thompson recalls, "It was partially my assignment that we were to be on Casper a lot on one-on-one coverage. I thought I had a great game. I know I was excited the whole game. I do remember us being very comfortable and handling them quite well most of the day."

Denver had led the NFL in rushing defense during the regular season, and the unit was true to form in holding the Raiders under 100 yards, while also limiting Stabler to just 215 passing yards.

The hitting was fierce on both sides, and Denver held a slim 7-3 margin at halftime, but Thompson's defense forced two pivotal second-half turnovers. The Broncos took advantage of those two turnovers to win their second game in three meetings with the Raiders that year. Defensive end Brison Manor recovered Oakland running back Clarence Davis' fumble at the Oakland 17, and Denver fullback Jon Keyworth scored from the one to increase the margin to 14-3 in the third quarter.

Oakland scored just 39 seconds into the final period to make the score 14-10, but on the next possession, Denver linebacker Bob Swenson intercepted a Stabler pass and ran to the Raiders' 14. A 12-yard TD strike from Craig Morton to wide receiver Haven Moses closed out the scoring.

"After all those years of losing, the feeling we had on the field is indescribable, and I know the fans felt the same way. We had beaten the Raiders. We were going to the Super Bowl. And nobody was ever going to call us losers again," Thompson recalls, with those words resonating for an entire state.

In the game of his life against Oakland on January 1, 1978, Billy Thompson and Denver's Orange Crush defense held the defending world champions to 17 points as the Broncos earned a trip to Super Bowl XII.
Courtesy of the Denver Broncos

The list of greatest games in Broncos history naturally starts with the first Super Bowl victory against Green Bay, and defeating Atlanta to become back-to-back champions one year later obviously jumps to the top as well. But any Broncos fan remembers the magical year when Denver made its mark and won for the first time, with the last road game scheduled as a trip to Super Bowl XII.

"There is no doubt in my mind about that," Thompson says. "That championship game turned everything around for the Broncos, and the city, and neither has ever been the same since then. I'm talking about perception and everything about this organization. People didn't really know what this organization was about. They didn't know anything about the players. Then, overnight, people actually started to see that this organization in a championship light, and we haven't looked back since."

Expectations for the Broncos were never the same after that game. "And rightfully so," the longtime captain adds. "I've always thought that coming in as a young player I wanted to win, and had always won where I had been before, and so I really didn't understand and was disappointed when we didn't win right away. But it taught me a lot of lessons about perseverance and hanging tough and doing the right things.

"Watching things happen, how you practice, how you play and how people look at you, those were critical things for me. It was really an experience for me to go through the times when we didn't win. And then we started to win, how meaningful it was to be a part of it—something special like that."

AFTER THE CHEERING STOPPED

His Ring of Fame induction came in 1987 and was no surprise to anyone, as he is arguably the best defensive back in team history. His career spanned 13 seasons with the Broncos, the first Denver player to be with the team that long, and he still ranks second in games started over a career with 178. The three-time Pro Bowler was a natural selection for this honor, but his focus was on continuing to move forward.

Thompson worked in private business for several years after his illustrious career ended, then returned to the Broncos, initially as a scout before settling into what is now his role as director of alumni relations/community relations. That involves getting former alumni who still live in the Denver area involved in the team's community relations outreach—an initiative in which the franchise is very aggressive.

Thompson explains, "We have quite a few guys who still live here in Colorado, and what we really do is act as ambassadors for the organization and bridge the gap to the community. Especially when active players are really busy during the season and don't have the time to be out in the community because of job constraints. It's a job that I really enjoy doing because out of all the things that have happened to me in my career here in Colorado, one thing that has never changed is the fan support for this organization. I'm thankful that I can give something back to the fans."

Most recently, he has become very active as the team's ambassador in the Broncos' work with the Boys and Girls Club of Denver, going full circle back to that time when he had some of his first athletic experiences as a youth spending time at those clubs in Chicago. "That's why it is so special to me. It's something that I really have a soft spot in my heart for, and when the Broncos had a chance to get involved with them I was really excited about it because I know what they do, and the programs that they offer to kids there are incredible."

He can be found at the club just about every Wednesday night talking with kids, helping with homework, reading a book or playing pool with them.

BT, The Captain, is no longer wearing number 36 and delivering hits from his safety position, but Billy Thompson has gone from roaming the secondary to being a captain in community work for the Denver Broncos.

"I know how much influence it can have on a kid. It means a lot to me and it is something that I intend on doing for a long time."

Chapter 11

GENE MINGO

BEFORE THE BRONCOS

In the case of Gene Mingo, before the Broncos means before just about everything, because he was among the few there at the very beginning—at the start of the American Football League. But he also was one of very few players with no college experience at all, and beyond that, was the first black placekicker in pro football history.

Thus, Mingo was a pioneer on several fronts, and it's safe to describe his situation as one that did not exactly involve opportunity knocking at his door. The 1950s were a different time in America, and Mingo was among those who paved the way.

He grew up in the tough part of Akron, Ohio, and recalls, "I hadn't graduated from elementary school, my mother was very ill, and my dad said, 'Son, you just keep getting into trouble. You don't like going to school. Why don't you stay home and take care of your mother?'"

Mingo did, and says, "In those almost three years that I stayed out of elementary school taking care of my mother, she taught me how to wash, iron, cook, sew—do all of the domestic stuff that a wife or mother is supposed to do. She had seven heart attacks and five strokes. When she passed away I said to her when we were viewing her body, I cried and said, 'Mom, I will never hurt another person again,' because I felt that if I had been that good little boy, then my mother would have been around a lot longer. I promised her that I was going to go back to school and be a good boy."

He went back to finish school—elementary school—and then on to high school where he was big, but not a player. During those three years that he was out taking care of his mother, his playmates were limited to the neighborhood's big boys. "I had learned quite a bit and gotten fairly tough doing that."

Whenever he ran into the football coach he would boast about his skills, and the young Mingo was reminded of that when he finally got to high school. One day coach Gordon Larson spotted the young braggart walking down the hallway and said, "You're the young man who always told me you're going to play on my football team. Practice has started, why haven't you come out?" Mingo tried to back away, but the coach grabbed him by the shoulder, took him down to the equipment room and told the trainer to get him into some gear. From then on, Gene Mingo had a new identity as a football player.

He was already a tough kid, older than many of his teammates, and his presence was felt on the high school fields around Akron.

But classroom work was another matter, and during his junior year Mingo left high school to join the navy.

Throughout football history, talent has been observed in lots of different ways, and how he came to play ball in the navy is about as crazy as passing a loaf of bread. The strapping young sailor was sent to Oceania Naval Air Station, where he was assigned to work in the cafeteria. "We were throwing around fresh cooked loaves of bread, and the chief cook came out and raised hell with us. He said, 'Do you

---

The first African-American placekicker in pro football, Gene Mingo also returned a punt 76 yards against the AFL Boston Patriots for the winning touchdown in the game of his life on September 9, 1960. *Courtesy of the Denver Broncos*

think you can play football? If you want to play football, I'll send you to a place where you can play football,'" Mingo recalls with laughter. After the cook's tirade, young Mingo was transferred. "I was sent down to a place called Little Creek Amphibious Base. It was a submarine base that had a football team. We were called the Little Creek Gators. Most of the guys I played with on that navy team were either All-American or had played college ball, and we even had a few pros."

This was a time in American history when most healthy young men performed military service, and pro athletes were no exceptions to the rule. Mingo flourished in this new environment, honing his skills against top-flight service teams.

"Playing in the service, when you go against the marines, army, or even another navy team, it was almost like playing against the Raiders or the Chiefs." The rosters were heavily stocked with former college and even pro players; the competition was fierce. "That's where I got most of my experience, playing service ball against Quantico, Camp Lejeune, Fort Belmar, Fort Dix."

He got out of the navy just after New Year's Day in 1959 and went to work at the Goodyear rim plant back in Akron.

THE SETTING

Mingo settled in at the rim plant, a long way from being the hero of the first game of a new pro football league. But he had tasted football and knew there was a living to be made outside of Akron. So he embarked on a letter-writing campaign that included one to Broncos general manager Dean Griffing. Griffing had seen Mingo play in service games and remembered his talent and versatility and opted to send Mingo a contract for $6,500.

No discussion of the setting for that first game can take place without a look at that first training camp for that first season.

"There is no imaginable comparison to be made," Mingo explains, looking for the right words to explain football as no current Broncos fan can even begin to imagine it. "I will always remember the first few days of practice. We were up in Golden, at the Colorado School of

GENE MINGO AT A GLANCE

POSITION: Halfback/Kicker
COLLEGE: No College
PLAYING HEIGHT, WEIGHT: 6-2, 216
YEARS PLAYED FOR BRONCOS: 1960-1964
UNIFORM NUMBER: 21
NOTABLE: The first African-American placekicker in pro football history, Gene Mingo led the American Football League in scoring in 1960 (123 points) and 1962 (1 37 points). He also led the AFL in field goals made in 1960 (18) and 1962 (27, at that time the pro football record). Mingo played in the 1962 AFL All-Star game.
THE GAME: Denver at Boston, September 9, 1960

Mines gymnasium. We had army cots in that gym with about 125 guys in there trying to make the Broncos football team. And we didn't have much equipment."

Mingo's description would defy belief if it was not known to be so. How much equipment is "not much"?

"We had one set of dumbbell bars and then (trainer) Fred Posey would put together buckets of cement and put steel rods through them for us to lift weights. That's what we had. When I tell people that, they don't even understand or believe that. We had one trainer taping all the ankles, trying to take care of everybody. We had one horse trough that was made into a whirlpool bath."

This was the environment in which Mingo was trying to climb out of the factories and neighborhoods of Akron, without the benefit of having played in college. And the versatile halfback was also the only black kicker in football. "There were a lot of taboos in pro football back in 1960, and it was harder for a black man."

The 1960 Denver Broncos official team picture shows five original Broncos were black players on that team for opening day, and one of the first road games was a preseason contest against the Dallas Texans in Little Rock, Arkansas.

As they got off the bus to go out on the field in Little Rock, some white guys were bluntly rude to the Broncos' black players. Mingo says, "They used the 'n' word, and were pretty rough—'If you hit one of those white boys, we're going to shoot you, we're going to lynch you.' We played the game without any incidents, but still, something like that never leaves your mind."

The final score of that game was 48-0 Dallas, and the Broncos were on their way to a 0-5 exhibition record.

The Broncos' hardscrabble training camp was coupled with an exhibition schedule that had them on the road for all five games. Given their surroundings, it was no surprise that they lost all five games, but the scores just added a new level of ignominy: They were outscored in exhibition play by a 192-53 margin, including a 43-6 embarrassment to opening-day opponent Boston in Providence.

Denver certainly was the laughingstock of the new league, and now the team headed to Boston to play the Patriots on a Friday night in the first official American Football League game.

Only by the chance of schedule did this landmark game feature the Broncos.

THE GAME OF MY LIFE

"Nobody could have touched me on September 9, 1960, when we played Boston. Here's a kid who did not even graduate high school and now he's starting a pro career that nobody really expected him to have, let alone score the winning touchdown on a punt return. That can never be broken."

Mingo had made the team as a halfback and placekicker, but he could run and could be used in an emergency as a return man on special teams.

The first game in AFL history was played at Boston University Field on a warm September night with 21,597 mostly curious spectators. The Patriots had the benefit of playing in a college setting, with full-time groundskeepers. Mingo recalls, "It was the best field I had ever played on. It was like walking on a carpet, but softer, it was so well groomed."

The Broncos admired the turf, but the crowd did not admire the Broncos. Their first-year uniforms were so notorious that today a pair of socks from that first season resides in the Pro Football Hall of Fame. The pants were brown, the jerseys were mustard (home) and white (road) and the socks were vertically striped, like the pole outside a barbershop.

"We had those vertical socks on, and when we went out on to the field for warm-ups the crowd just went wild. They started to laugh at us—'Here come the clowns. Look at those clowns,'" Mingo recollects.

But it was still pro football, the start of a monumental new era, and the laughter did not mean much to anybody lucky enough to be in one of those atrocious suits. Denver had lost every preseason game, and expectations were below minimal for the fledgling Broncos.

Boston scored first on a field goal, but Denver's ageless quarterback, Frank Tripucka, connected on a second-quarter scoring pass to NFL veteran halfback Al Carmichael, and the first halftime in AFL history showed a 7-3 Bronco advantage.

Mingo was not scheduled to see any action as a return man in that game, but the Denver kick returners had sustained first-half injuries at their regular positions. At the end of the half, head coach Frank Filchock approached Mingo, saying: "Mingo, you're running back punts and kickoffs."

Mingo was not expecting that. "I was so nervous and scared," he remembers.

Jim Greer, one of the Denver receivers, reached over and said, "Hey man, don't be nervous. Just do it like you do in practice. Catch the ball and run." Other players lent their support as well. Mingo remembers it well. "The black players came over to me and gave me some encouragement. I was scared, but I was excited too."

Late in the third quarter, Boston took a 10-7 lead, and on their next possession the Patriots were forced to punt. Mingo caught it at the Denver 24, and took off.

"I can still see it now. I made like I was making a move to my left, then back to my right. I picked up my blockers and just ran down the sideline. When I got there, I was so tired that I couldn't kick the extra point. I kicked a big divot out of the ground. My leg was dead.

"When Frank Filchock told me at halftime that I was going to be running back punt returns and kickoffs, I was scared you-know-whatless. But when I caught that punt, and was going down our sideline and I could see Filchock and some of the guys waving me on, that was one of the best feelings. There's no way to describe it. To get down there and not knowing at that time that it was going to be the winning points, it was just wonderful."

In fact, that 76-yard punt-return touchdown, the first in AFL history, held up and was the winning factor in the first-ever game played by two franchises that both would go on to Super Bowl immortality decades later.

And it was just the first game in what would become an 11-year pro football career touched by history, for Mingo stands alone as the first African-American plackekicker in pro football.

But for Gene Mingo on that perfect New England night in September, the streets of Akron were far away and that moment in time would live on forever.

AFTER THE CHEERING STOPPED

Gene Mingo worked for many post-football years, and he's trying to be retired, but it's not easy. He has the kind of experience that is only garnered by being there, and his counseling skills are in high demand.

It's been a long time since his career ended, but Mingo remains active today in the Denver area as an alcohol and drug counselor, specializing in intervention work.

"They call me and I talk to the family members, get them together, to work out a plan to confront this person in what is called an intervention. These are the things that inspire me today and keep me going," Mingo says. "Doing intervention work is not pleasant, it's very draining on not only me, but the family that is performing it. That's what I do."

He points out that a lot of people will not go to anyone else and share when they have a problem. He becomes that stranger who hopefully helps to turn their lives around.

Mingo is also active in the Denver Broncos Alumni Association. "I have traveled a long route. I understand what football players go through and know how sometimes there are people out there who are trying to influence players in a great number of ways, not all of them positive. I've got the experience to help them understand what happens after football, and I would always be open to talking about these situations, if it were ever necessary."

Mingo realizes that there are a number of support systems in place for the modern player, but just as he was called upon to return punts at halftime of that first game, he remains ready to step into any situation for his old team.

"I have had a lot of good things happen in my life, and I'll always be a Bronco."

Chapter 12

HAVEN MOSES

BEFORE THE BRONCOS

Haven Moses not only was a player before the scouts knew it, he was a player before he knew it himself.

He was a natural at football, but it would be a while before it mattered.

His young life revolved around family and education in south central Los Angeles, growing up in an area that was a good place to grow up back in the day, before it became known to the police and sociologists simply as South Central.

"We didn't have a lot. We didn't know that, and the struggles were like what most people had. Growing up, I didn't realize I was in the first class of the baby boom era, with veterans coming back. And at the same time a lot of African Americans were migrating to California from the south, and other areas where there was perceived opportunity. Nothing was stopping the development and opportunity post-war, and it was a wonderful period of time in the growth of our country. That was my era, and my folks did a great job of nurturing us kids."

Moses had 12 years of Catholic education and says nothing could replace the discipline and structure that his young life was given. "My parents felt if I was in that environment, I would have a better chance to focus on the opportunity, skills that would help address a future career. Building one's foundation, one's character, is everything. You grow to be responsible, with respect and manners.

"Going to schools outside my community allowed me to see firsthand those things that were attainable, and that my parents were preparing me to have a chance to be a part of the American dream."

Moses notes that perhaps no other area in the country was as alive with the American dream as post-war southern California.

"Baseball was my first love, that being my first exposure to professional sports, since my mother and grandmother were from the south, where Negro baseball was huge. Any thought I had of playing sports beyond Little League that I might have had at that time were certainly toward baseball, due to the prominence of those individuals."

Moses didn't play organized football until his freshman year of high school. But once he started, there was no looking back.

"Going into high school, I had to learn how to put a jock on. But nice things started to happen to me in high school athletics. It was a wonderful carryover from my youth. Without undue pressure, we kept playing, and I began to be a part of teams that won. We won our school's first CIF title (the California equivalent of a state high school championship); but being at a small high school, whatever I accomplished paled in comparison to the fame received by the kids at far larger high schools, especially in a city the size of LA."

So when graduation time came, no athletic scholarship offers came Moses' way. The rich lode of talent in Southern California made him anonymous to college recruiters, and with education always number

Haven Moses, the second half of Denver's famous "M & M Connection," was a stellar receiver with the team for the best 10 years of his career. *Rich Clarkson/Denver Broncos*

one in his household, he had little interest in even attending the year-end senior sports banquet.

But good luck always seems to reward the hard working and diligent.

"My mother talked me into going, and there was a junior college coach there named Floyd 'Scrappy' Rhea. He was beating the bushes for kids who were not going to be Division I kids."

Rhea told Moses he could get him into Los Angeles Harbor Junior College. Moses accepted with the idea of attending, then getting a job in the real world for which he had been prepared.

"He got me into Harbor, and that's when the story began. We went undefeated two years in a row—JC national champs two years in a row. We were a real light and scrappy team."

Moses was just playing, using his natural skills, and he was unaware that it was all getting bigger than that. They won two JC bowl games and the lithe youngster was a JC All-American two years in a row as a defensive back.

At the time, yet-to-be-legendary coach Don Coryell was scouting players from San Diego City College for his school, San Diego State.

Moses recalls a bizarre turn of events. "We played them, and he just happened to watch some film of Harbor. We had two receivers go down. I was a DB, but Scrappy said, 'We need a decoy. Get out there and play wide receiver.' The ball was not supposed to come to me, but our quarterback saw me standing out there, no experience, one-on-one. He threw two passes, two TDs—both 60 or 70 yards."

That quarterback was future number-one draft choice Don Horn. Horn transferred to State; he talked to Don Coryell, and from that conversation Moses received a scholarship to San Diego State.

"I didn't know it at the time, but my preparation for my life and career in Denver was taking shape, and it was all about character and winning."

Indeed, Moses had played on his high school's first championship team, then at Harbor JC had made All-America as an integral member of two straight national championship teams. He followed that up at San Diego State, where they were small-school national champs two

HAVEN MOSES AT A GLANCE

POSITION: Wide Receiver
COLLEGE: San Diego State University
PLAYING HEIGHT, WEIGHT: 6-2, 208
YEARS PLAYED FOR BRONCOS: 1972-1981
UNIFORM NUMBER: 25
NOTABLE: A 1988 inductee into the Denver Broncos Ring of Fame, Haven Moses played 10 seasons for the Broncos and ranks eighth among all Broncos in career receptions (302) and receiving yards (5,450). He had 44 touchdown receptions and a yards-per-catch average of 18.0. Moses was inducted into the Colorado Sports Hall of Fame in 1986 along with fellow member of the "M St M Connection," quarterback Craig Morton.
THE GAME: Oakland at Denver, January 1, 1978

years in a row. Moses earned five titles in five years, at three different levels of play.

"I was team captain of the 1967 national champion team. Looking back, I was a winner at every stage of my development, but I didn't pay attention to any of that at the time. The environment made Haven Moses. Playing for Scrappy, he took interest in me. He saw something special. They were all relatively small schools, but I began to realize I was in something where I could be comfortable and do very well. I never allowed myself to think I was better than what I was focusing on at that time. There are guys on the street corner right now who are better, faster, stronger, quicker, what have you; but there is something that separates those who take it to the next level from those who remain where they are, with just the athletic talent.

"Teams are not entirely comprised of guys who always grab the headlines; there are other individuals who make just as much of an impact on the game."

But he was both—a high-impact, skilled position player with a complete concept of team first, team always.

"In reflection it was all just unbelievable."

Drafted ninth by the Buffalo Bills in the first round, he played four years for Buffalo before a 1972 trade sent him back west, to a Denver Broncos team that would not experience its first winning season as a franchise until 1973.

THE SETTING

The Broncos were lousy.

But head coach John Ralston and personnel chiefs Fred Gehrke and Carroll Hardy were quickly building a quantum change in both talent and attitude on that Denver squad.

Moses recalls, "It started with the talent that they brought in—individually talented players, but collectively, not only talented but team players, very solid. Just like my previous situations: talented, but also very good people at the same time.

"The nucleus of a team is shaped within its atmosphere," Moses says pointedly, "and we began to look at ourselves as winners."

The Broncos went 7-5-2 in 1973, the first winning season ever. They followed that up with two more winning seasons in the next three years.

"We realized, 'Hey, we have a group of guys here who have won before, and are talented winners.' We knew there was something here."

In 1976, when the Broncos fell short of the playoffs, a lot of frustration set in, with the pervasive feeling that the team was better than the record. Ultimately, Red Miller replaced Ralston as head coach.

"The foundation was large, and it was set. Ralston being ousted could have torn this team apart; however, it didn't. And that situation strengthened the bond, and that was not going to be a distraction. We were going to do what we had the capabilities of doing. Red came in, made some key adjustments, and let us play.

"Red was the right coach at the right time, much of the major puzzle had been put into place, and the players truly bonded, rallied, and said, 'OK, we are that good.' It was a team of destiny. From the ashes of the previous off-season, this team came together in training camp. We were focused on reaching our potential, whatever that might have been. We wanted to get out on the field and prove ourselves."

It all came together for Denver in 1977. From the first game against Don Coryell's St. Louis Cardinals, the Broncos played like a true team of destiny. They rolled to an eventual 12-2 record, winning their first AFC Western Division title. They clinched a playoff berth—another first for the organization—and eventually settled into the surreal, seemingly unbelievable position as the top seed in the entire AFC.

Broncos fans rode the euphoria of Broncomania into the playoffs. People painted their cars and houses orange, and the nightly news reported a daily stream of orange-induced behavior that you had to see to believe.

Orange toilet seats? You could buy them in Denver. Want ads listed by color? You could find them in Denver.

The team enjoyed every moment of it, but Moses points out, "We really did play one game at a time. We kept marching down that path with a quiet confidence. Nothing was said, we just went about our business, pretty much flying under the radar nationally."

Moses and his Broncos teammates were having a dynamic impact on the community. He remembers it well, and with tearful emotion. "The fans were working themselves up into a frenzy. All of a sudden, we were getting positive national attention. They and their team were no longer regarded as jokes. These great fans, who had put up with national abuse and scorn directed to their team over years and years, were rewarded. With those two playoff games here in Denver, for the first time ever—and to me this is the greatest thing about that year— we treated our fans to those two games. We brought those games home to our fans, and they were able to witness firsthand something really special.

"We were part of our fan base. Our locker room was in the south stands, and we did not have private player parking. We had to work our way through our fans. The motor homes would be lined up right behind player parking, and they came early and stayed late to tailgate. Often we would go out after the games into the RVs, have a beer, a hot dog, and just spend time talking with our fans. That relationship was special, between the fans and the players.

"What we did, it was for them as much as us."

The two teams that came into Mile High Stadium were dominating the 1970s. After all, the Raiders were the defending world champions and Pittsburgh was in the midst of winning four titles in six years.

But on Christmas Eve 1977, the Steelers lost to the Broncos in Denver 34-21. After the game, Pittsburgh quarterback Terry Bradshaw, assessing the fan frenzy within the stadium, said, "It will never be like this again. There is nothing like the first time a team wins."

So just like that, Pittsburgh was out, and the Raiders were coming.

But Moses recollects, "We were still under the radar. Sportswriters didn't give us much of a chance against the Raiders, but as we had progressed through the season, our confidence grew more and more. The locker room was unbelievably loose the whole year, and we were sky high for that championship game. We were a family, there were no barriers; we came together and worked together. There was nothing divisive on that football team."

The camaraderie on the 1977 team mirrored those teams on which Moses had honed his skills—those championship teams at every level. The Ring of Fame receiver notes, "It was a real team—individual talents, yes, but individuals who came together and had the respect and character that everyone brought into it. This allowed us to max out our individual abilities.

"We really began to realize the impact of what was going on. The history we were about to make was not lost on us."

THE GAME OF MY LIFE

Denver quarterback Craig Morton was hurt. He had gotten beat up pretty badly in the playoff game against the Steelers the previous week, and the team didn't know who was going to be playing quarterback. Backup Norris Weese had taken the snaps all week. "We just went about our business," Moses remembers. "Nobody ever said anything expressing concern. We didn't really talk to Craig that whole week. He was in the hospital and the team was trying to keep that information from the Raiders. I had never in my life seen anything like the left side of his body; it was so black and blue."

The team practiced like it had all year, one practice at a time. "We became more intense as the week moved along, but it did not seem stressful. The Raiders probably were saying, 'Hey, they have never been here before. This is a big game. They don't have championship experience; they'll buckle under pressure.' But this team was poised the whole year. And we had played in some big games to get there. There were many times along the way when we could have folded, but we didn't."

The Broncos had had a terrible history at home against the Raiders, but the entire city could sense that things were different for this game on New Year's Day 1978.

Still, the defending champions were formidable in every way, featuring a cast of stars and future Hall of Famers, including head coach John Madden. Moses says in reflection that it required great focus to stay with the task at hand. "They had some unbelievable players. But in their minds, I think they thought we would fold under the pressure. Even though we had played them twice and beaten them once in the regular season, this was on the big stage. We had not been there before, and perhaps in John Madden's mind, he thought he could come in and kind of intimidate us.

"But we were at home. We were with our families, and with our fans. We were going to bring something special to this city, and we knew it. We just had this quiet confidence about ourselves."

The Raiders scored on their initial possession as Errol Mann kicked a 20-yard field goal to end an 18-play, 54-yard drive at 10:34 of the first quarter. But the Broncos' "M & M Connection" of Morton and Moses hooked up just two plays later on a 74-yard scoring pass. The Broncos had utilized a very balanced attack the whole year, and a lot of their success was about the defense—the "Orange Crush"—but the offense was capable of striking suddenly.

"A lot of our game plans were built around making sure we did not put the defense in bad situations. But this was the one time that the offense was the catalyst for the whole thing. Craig hit me on that first play. It was short motion, a corner route. When I beat (cornerback) Skip Thomas on that, at first I thought it was just for the first down, but Skip made a mistake, thought my momentum was pushing me out of bounds. I saw space between me and the end zone downfield, and when I just felt a slight tap on my shoulder from Skip, I turned that sucker up and took off. By the time I got to about the five-yard line, I turned around to look for flags. I saw no flags, and that was the beginning of a great day. We buckled down offensively, and we just played football."

That 7-3 lead held up through the rest of the first half, with both defenses stifling the rival offenses.

Denver took advantage of two costly Oakland turnovers to increase its lead in the second half. The Broncos recovered an Oakland fumble at the Raiders 17, and running back Jon Keyworth scored from the one to give Denver a 14-3 margin at 6:23 of the third period.

Oakland quarterback Ken Stabler hit tight end Dave Casper on a seven-yard touchdown pass with just 39 seconds left in the third quarter, and the Broncos were left holding onto a 14-10 advantage as the fourth stanza began.

But on Oakland's next possession, linebacker Bob Swenson intercepted a Stabler pass and ran to the Raiders 14. Moses was a big-play guy throughout his career, and he had another huge catch coming in this game.

Two plays later, Morton and Moses struck again, this time for 12 yards and Denver's final score, giving Denver a 20-10 advantage with 7:17 remaining.

It was a spectacular diving catch by Moses, who hauled in the ball just inches off the ground in the middle of the end zone. "The second touchdown catch came on a broken play. I was his third receiver. The south end zone was muddy and rock hard. Craig was going to two of the other receivers first, then looked at me. I was stumbling around, trying to get away from Lester Hayes. Craig threw the ball low, and as I was falling, I did not have my feet underneath me, but had to steady my body to let the ball come into my arms. I had to catch it with that 'pocket' that I made, rather than let myself slam into the ground, because I was going down pretty fast."

Oakland finished the scoring on the next series with another Stabler-to-Casper pass, but Denver then controlled the ball for the final 3:08. The Broncos were on their way to Super Bowl XII, sending the Mile High City into whatever lies beyond ecstasy.

One of the most highly respected Broncos ever, Moses always had perspective—an understanding of how things tie together. "Every organization has to have a cornerstone, has to have a foundation, and you can't forget what it takes to start something. To me, from that year, the Broncos have been a successful franchise from that moment on— a premiere franchise. And that's the pride that we all have in being there at the time.

"It was a remarkable game. Personally, for me, it helped me to validate my career. I had played well at all my previous levels, and all that work and determination paid off finally. I had four catches, two for touchdowns—our first and last TDs of the game. But not giving up was the most important thing. I had a picture of my mother and father in my mind, and of all the people who over the years had believed in me as an individual. It was about doing well as a person, more than doing well as an athlete."

The Broncos and their fans had been vindicated at last by winning that first championship.

"You can't replicate that. That game was representative of the entire 1977 season. The whole place was just orange. It is hard to express what a special season, year, and game it was.

"The fans were on the field with us that day, and we respected their patience and their loyalty. To be able to give them something for the first time, that was the highlight of my life."

It was still very early time in Denver's major-league sports history, but nothing for Denver and the Broncos would ever be the same again.

"This city came together, in terms of greatness. Look at this city, what it has become, and the Broncos' success has lent directly to the national recognition of Denver."

AFTER THE CHEERING STOPPED

After a 14-year pro career—10 of those years in Denver—with 448 overall receptions, 57 touchdowns and over 8,000 yards, Haven Moses retired.

But just from football, not from life.

"Everything I have achieved in life, professionally and personally, is because of that foundation of understanding of respect, of being part of something that is not individual. My parents instilled that and so it just got stronger and stronger because I was in environments, on teams, that were not recognized, and allowed me to develop. I played in an era when teams were truly teams. Everything reinforced my upbringing. There were a lot of people like myself, who could make things happen as a group. And in retirement, I knew I still wanted to be part of a team, moving a little part of society forward one step at a time."

A Denver resident since being traded from Buffalo in 1972, Haven and his wife, Joyce, have continued to make their home in the Mile High City, where he currently works with a private school called the Excel Institute in the Park Hill neighborhood.

Before that, Moses worked for a Denver-based luggage manufacturing firm for four years in its management training program, then embarked on a 15-year second career with Denver's Coors Brewing Company.

"I actually worked for Coors for one more year than I played in the NFL, and it was great," Moses recalls. "But I really had a great urge to work with groups that helped kids." He joined the Archdiocese of Denver after leaving Coors.

As always, his sincerity is absolute. "My focus there is on inner-city education. Family, support of family, and education are the elements that provide the support and foundation in life, along with your spiritual faith as well. When you get to that point, education allows you to pull those elements together, to develop as a young man or woman, and it gives you those tools to be able to maximize the opportunities life affords.

"The world is a lot better now than it was several generations ago. There continue to be struggles, but it is the preparation in life that helps you face those issues and move on."

Moses remains involved in organizations such as the Boys and Girls Clubs, but there is a common denominator. "The organizations that I have been involved in are geared toward youth, and helping kids."

His life took a sad turn on January 9, 2003, when Moses had a stroke. The recovery was slow, but steady, and he credits his family and innumerable friends for their unfailing support as he made his recovery.

Moses reflected on his life and beliefs, saying, "It is not what you do as much as the substance of who you are. I am most proud of the fact that I was able to use negative things as encouragement to do positive things. How we learn from and respond to the things that happen to us is most important. I want to help kids to understand that it is one thing to have potential, but you must learn what it is going to take to overcome roadblocks and challenges.

"How one is able to adapt and adjust is very important. Good people do finish first."

Chapter 13

CRAIG MORTON

BEFORE THE BRONCOS

When Craig Morton entered the room, everyone noticed. He was one of those guys.

Morton was a sports golden boy in California—a major star in high school football and baseball and an All-America quarterback at the University of California.

When the National Football League Dallas Cowboys drafted him in the first round, it was just another step in the natural progression for someone exuding star power.

"I played three sports at Campbell High School—football, basketball, and baseball. I was good at all of them and could have played any one of them in college. I chose football and baseball in college and ended up choosing football," Morton points out.

He could do it all, but an incident in his second year at Cal made him a pocket passer forever. Morton recalls, "When I was a sophomore in college, the first day in full practice, coach Marv Levy had me returning punts. I had done that all through high school, of course.

The whole punt team versus just two guys trying to return punts full go. I lasted about three or four times and then just tore my knee—one of the real stupid things that happened. But then they wanted to redshirt me, and I said no. I probably came back too soon. I played the last five games of my sophomore year, and then the rest of the other two years. But that's how I hurt my knee, returning punts."

A center fielder who decided completing passes happens more frequently that hitting a baseball, he settled on football at Cal. "I chose to go out for spring practice my senior year," he recalls. "We had a new coach, and he set the condition that if I didn't go to spring practice I couldn't be team captain, and that was one of my goals. So I did that and played my senior year, was drafted number one by the Cowboys and was behind Don Meredith for three years.

"It was my fourth year when I was up in northern California with some of my friends, vacationing on the Russian River, and I heard on the radio that Meredith had retired and I was the quarterback."

But Roger Staubach was a Cowboy as well. "Roger and I had played against each other in college our senior years, and we beat Navy, which was a big accomplishment. I had no idea what things were to come with Roger's competitiveness and mine pitted against one another."

Morton was starting at quarterback and playing extremely well, but separated his shoulder in his second season as the Dallas starter. "Roger was ready, but I kept playing with the separated right shoulder, which was a big mistake. I played the whole year with the shoulder like that. Then all the ligaments became damaged, and I had to have a doctor transplant a tendon into my right shoulder. I developed some elbow problems because of that. My history with the Cowboys is that I did take them to their first Super Bowl. But the next year, Coach Landry decided that the job was open, we went back and forth, and he awarded the job to Roger. We went to the Super Bowl again and

Veteran quarterback Craig Morton joined the Broncos in 1977 and made an immediate impact. He was named AFC Most Valuable Player and led Denver to its first playoff appearance.
Rod Hanna/Denver Broncos

won. The next year, we were in competition again. He had said that it was open again. We competed and Roger got hurt, and then I played the whole year."

The Cowboys defeated San Francisco in the divisional game. "Roger came in in the last two minutes and won the game for us. That's the only time he played the whole year—amazing comeback."

Staubach's amazing comeback signaled the end for Morton in Dallas. He remembers, "It was evident that one of us had to go, so I just said, 'I'm not going to do this anymore.'"

Both quarterbacks were known as fierce competitors, and both wanted to start. Morton ultimately was traded to the New York Giants, which at that time was at a low ebb for the historic franchise.

Morton remembers, "It was just a bad situation, and in the summer of 1977 I got a call from the Giants telling me they were sorry, but I had been traded to the Denver Broncos. I said, 'God, thank you very, very much,' because I knew the Broncos had a great defense. I said, 'Boy, if they had a quarterback, this could be a really good team.' Well, we got a new quarterback, me, and a new coach, Red Miller."

THE SETTING

"Nineteen seventy-seven was the magical year that started Denver on the playoff ride with the Orange Crush and put Denver on the map as an exceptional football city. That kind of changed the whole scenario of sports and what people thought about football in Denver," according to Morton. But there had been no prelude to suggest what was about to happen.

Craig Morton, the natural, the golden boy who had now been banged around by injury and circumstances, had another chance. This time with a new coach and a franchise that was on the cusp of national prominence. The Broncos had been 9-5 in 1976, and the feeling was very strong that "if they only had a quarterback…"

"The first time I went to Denver, I walked in the locker room and (defensive end) Lyle Alzado was sitting there. He was the only guy in

CRAIG MORTON AT A GLANCE

POSITION: Quarterback
COLLEGE: University of California
PLAYING HEIGHT, WEIGHT: 6-4, 214
YEARS PLAYEDFOR BRONCOS: 1977-82
UNIFORM NUMBER: 7
NOTABLE: A 1988 inductee into the Denver Broncos Ring of Fame, Craig Morton led the Broncos to their first Super Bowl berth in Super Bowl XII. He earned a variety of awards for his 1977 performance with the Broncos, including AFC Most Valuable Player. He led the Broncos to divisional titles in 1977 and 1978. Morton was inducted into the Colorado Sports Hall of Fame in 1986, along with fellow member of the "M &M Connection," wide receiver Haven Moses.
THE GAME: Oakland at Denver, January 1, 1978

the room at the time, and I walked in there to kind of look at the locker room. He looked at me and said, 'Now we'll win a championship,' which was a great comment that I'll certainly never forget. Lyle and I were really good friends. He was a great player, as was that defense. But nothing was promised to me when I came to the Broncos."

It did not take long for Morton to distance himself from Denver's other quarterbacks when training camp started. Head coach Red Miller knew his defense was powerful, his offensive nucleus was good, and he liked veteran signal callers.

"There was really nothing but the Broncos," Morton remembers, "and the stadium was being enlarged for the final time when I got there, which was a big deal for the city because the people liked their Broncos, but didn't have high expectations. They certainly didn't think I was going to come in and do anything special. But they knew they had a pretty good defense.

"I thought it was about time I just kind of rededicated my life and got back to what kind of quarterback I knew I could be."

Miller knew what he had in Morton, and their relationship was such that the quarterback was willing to let his arm play backup to the emerging defense that would carry the team.

Morton immediately became the man. The Broncos jumped out of the gate fast and finished 12-2, gaining a playoff berth and home-field advantage while helping the city coin the term "Broncomania."

But along the way, the bumps and bruises began to take their toll, with the worst of them being a nagging hip pointer. "Towards the end of the season, I kept getting worse and worse," recalls Morton. But he knew he had to play through it.

"My left hip started bleeding more and more. In the last game of the regular season we were going back to Dallas. Red had said, 'What do you think?' I said, 'You know, Coach, I'd like to maybe rest my hip here because it keeps exploding.' It had started to calm down and going into the playoffs, it would've been nice to have a week of rest. He said, 'Why don't you just kind of make an appearance, play a series or two?' I said, 'Well, OK.' But I got caught in a blitz, and it burst again, and I left the game."

The Broncos opened the playoffs with a home win over the Pittsburgh Steelers, Morton playing the whole game despite hurting his hip once again, this time sending the veteran QB to the hospital.

THE GAME OF MY LIFE

"When we talk about the game of my life, it is really the week of my life. Nothing like this had ever happened to me before. We're about to play for the right to go to the Super Bowl, and I had to go to the hospital because the hip pointer just started hemorrhaging, and my leg got about two inches filled with blood all over. It was just completely full with blood and nothing could happen.

"Not only did I have to go in, but I was there a week," Morton explains. It should be noted that one of the game's sidebars is that it changed the way injuries were reported in the NFL. The Broncos kept Morton's hospital stay a secret from the press all week, a policy no longer allowed, with the new policy created as a direct result of the Morton injury.

"I went in, and then I never practiced. I just stayed in the hospital. Red had practices closed. Nobody knew it. Jack Dolbin (Broncos wide receiver) was a chiropractor, and physicians frowned on him getting involved in my treatment, but hey, I needed to play. Jack would come to the hospital and perform a galvanic stimulation on me, which was the new machine, something he knew about because of being a chiropractor. He tried to get the blood circulating, and nothing was really working. Jack was doing treatment on me the previous weeks, and it helped a lot. I'd go over to his house and not tell any of the doctors anything because they thought it was quackery. But we did it anyhow, and it helped. Then when my leg got so full of blood, the only thing they tried to do was put needles in there and tried to extract the blood, but it wasn't working. This is all week long in the hospital.

"Red came and gave me the game plan on Wednesday, and we talked a little bit about it. Then, Haven Moses came over and talked a little bit about some of the patterns, some of the nuances we were going to try to do to take advantage of some of the things the Raiders were doing. We had already played them twice that year—we beat them at their place and then lost to them at home. We knew the Raiders well enough and I knew them well enough that I wasn't really worried about that.

"But I really didn't think I was going to play. I didn't have a clue because I couldn't even walk. I said, 'Boy, is this something? I get into this situation, and I'm not going to play.'"

This story reads like a surreal fairy tale to anyone familiar with pro football, but sometimes fairy tales have happy endings.

"Sunday morning it was very, very cold, but it was sunny. A friend of mine, Loren Hewley, who has been a lifelong friend, came to the hospital and picked me up. I got up and I could barely walk. I hadn't been up very much. He said, 'What are you thinking?' I said, 'I don't know if I can do this or not.' He said, 'You've worked your whole life to do this. You cannot afford not to play.' He said, 'You know, you just have to do this.' I said, 'Well, get me to the stadium.'

"So I went to the stadium pretty early and got in the whirlpool and just sat there for an hour and a half or so to get loose. During pregame I was on the training table, and they were treating me and trying to get this thing broken up a little more. And I stayed on the table on purpose, just lying there, because the leg was just completely black and blue. I mean it was just a horrible thing. It looked like it was just a terribly bruised, huge piece of meat. I was going to play, and I had to make sure everybody knew that I need some protection or it was going to be a horrible day.

"I heard comments from some of my teammates who said it was just the ugliest thing they had ever seen. Eventually I went to my locker and started putting my clothes on. I got my pants and everything on and sat in my chair, and I leaned over and I couldn't reach my feet. I couldn't tie my shoes. I got them on because I wiggled and wiggled and got them on, but I said, 'I can't bend over.' Red came over to me and said, 'What do you think?' And I said, 'Coach, if you can tie my shoes, I'll play.' So the head coach tied my shoes. I wonder if any quarterback has ever said that before for a championship game!

"I realized in pregame I could move backwards pretty well. I couldn't go forwards too well because I couldn't press off. But I could set up OK. I could do that adequately enough. I got in the huddle before the first play, and said, 'If they don't touch me, we'll win the game.' And the Raiders only hit me a couple times, and I landed on the other side. The line did a phenomenal job. The guys made great plays. The first pass I threw was kind of a 15, 17 route to Haven across the middle, and the free safety for Oakland, Jack Tatum, had it hit him on the chest but he did not catch it. It's a good thing he didn't catch that pass because it would've been a bit of trouble.

"The next time I ran it we were able to suck him in there, and we went to the corner and Haven went 74 yards for a touchdown. I told Haven, 'Go to the corner.' It was a corner route. 'We'll fake him out

Half of the Broncos' famed "M & M Connection," quarterback Craig Morton led Denver to their first Super Bowl berth in 1978, playing through the pain of a nagging hip pointer.
Rod Hanna/Denver Broncos

and we'll get him biting, and then it's open.' So Haven made a great route and I threw it and he ran down the sidelines, which was amazing."

That gave the Broncos a 7-3 lead, which they never relinquished. "From then on, we just played great defense. We got a great call on a handoff to Rob Lytle in the third quarter. Lytle fumbled, but the whistle had already blown. That was a great break for us. But I was standing right in front of the referee, Chuck Heberling, so of course he couldn't see the play, which was very fortunate. So he blew the whistle."

Two plays later fullback Jon Keyworth scored to expand the lead to 14-3. The Broncos' final score was on a 12-yard pass from Morton to Moses, a combo that had become known as the "M & M Connection" during that magical season. Oakland scored to make it 20-14. Morton remembers, "On the last drive we had to make a first down because they started coming back. I'll never forget that last running play for us, when (running back) Otis Armstrong's hand came up out of the mass of people and he had made the first down and had that No. 1 sticking up. That was phenomenal. The gun sounded, and people went berserk."

Morton had completed 10 of 20 for 224 yards with the two touchdowns. His leadership that day and that year made him the AFC's Most Valuable Player for 1977.

The fairy tale was over, the dreams had come true.

That was the first of Denver's six AFC championships, and while the franchise has been one of the NFL's premiere teams since, nothing is remembered like the first time.

This team had not been a winner, and Morton did something in the most extreme of physical circumstances that ties him forever to what this franchise has become.

"Although we didn't win the Super Bowl, that game was something that will never be duplicated, ever."

Denver historians would argue that only the two Super Bowl wins themselves are bigger than this game in the history of the Broncos and possibly in the history of the city, laying the foundation for the Mile High City's growth and confidence.

Morton proudly notes, "When we went to New Orleans for that Super Bowl, that's when the people of Denver really got their pride—pride that we're a big-league city."

AFTER THE CHEERING STOPPED

Morton's body always ached, and the inactivity of a work stoppage during the strike-shortened 1982 season led him to call it quits after an 18-year pro career.

Induction into the Broncos' Ring of Fame followed in 1988, and Morton has occupied himself with business ventures in his native California since he hung up the cleats.

But there is no love like your first love for a Cal guy.

"I finally got back to the university, where I've always wanted to be, to help them raise money," Morton says. His primary fundraising goal was for Cal's new football facility, which broke ground in December 2006 and opened in 2011.

"We will get to the stadium in the next part of the process, but this is 140,000 square feet of locker rooms, meeting rooms, and weight rooms, a medical center, and then room for 12 Olympic sports. It's a phenomenal project, and it's something that it's great to be a part of.

"I am just very content, very happy. It's my alma mater, and it's my home. It's a place I just love being a part of, a great place."

But Morton's ties with the Broncos are never ending.

"When the Broncos called back in 1983 and asked me what I thought about John Elway wearing number seven, I said, 'Well, he'll be in the Hall of Fame one day. He's got that much talent.' I laughed and said, 'Give it to him because that's the way number seven will get to the Hall of Fame.'"

Chapter 14

JACK DOLBIN

BEFORE THE BRONCOS

Cinderella isn't always a girl, and nice guys don't always finish last. Jack Dolbin's story is proof positive on both counts.

"Jack Dolbin could fly. He could block, play special teams, had great hands, was tough as nails, and he was a great football player," Denver Broncos head coach Red Miller said of Dolbin.

But before that—way before that—Dolbin was raised in the coal regions of central Pennsylvania, where the only choice was to grow up tough and master a work ethic early on. And when it came to work ethic, Jack Dolbin became a poster boy.

"I played coal region football, in that anthracite region of the state, which I am proud of."

Dolbin took a thick resume of high school athletic achievement with him to Wake Forest University. But he suffered some injuries that included a broken leg, and wasn't drafted by a pro team. But that just set up the rest of the story.

Consistent with his hard-scrabble background, Dolbin ended up playing his first year of professional football at the minor-league level with the Pottstown Firebirds, a legendary minor-league franchise which was immortalized by a book (*The Forgettables*) and an NFL Films production chronicling a Firebirds championship season featuring Dolbin.

Then his career got even tougher.

"The second year, I played with the Schuylkill County Coal Crackers, which was actually a couple steps below Pottstown as far as the level of competition.

"Back in the '70s teams were allowed to have a taxi squad, and the Philadelphia Eagles taxi team was sent up to Pottstown every week to play minor-league football. The idea was that you would get these five or six guys some experience. What was interesting to me was that the five or six guys the Eagles sent up couldn't play for the Pottstown Firebirds. They weren't good enough.

"A lot of guys on that team were very similar to me. Maybe judged an inch too short or a step too slow or maybe they had circumstances in college—as I did with injuries—where they just didn't get drafted." There were also people like Otis Sistrunk with the Norfolk Neptunes, who never went to college but forged his way into the NFL. It was a team of people, within a league of people, all judged to be too short, too small, too slow.

But it was an intermediate level of play that Dolbin feels is missing today, with the exception of the NFL Europe League. "Oftentimes people don't have the intermediate level. They don't have the training grounds that we had back in the late '60s, early '70s to get into the National Football League."

So Dolbin, a future starter on a Denver Broncos Super Bowl team, played a year for the Firebirds, and a year with the Coal Crackers, and then it got tougher still.

Jack Dolbin made three attempts at a professional football career before the Broncos signed him in 1975. He played in every game of his career until a knee injury forced him to hang up his cleats. *Courtesy of the Denver Broncos*

"I was out of football for two years. I had decided to go to chiropractic college, and the NFL had restructured their taxi system so there were no longer minor-league teams available. I had given it two years and didn't get any offers, so I went to chiropractic college in Chicago. I was working for JC Penney's as a security guard, chasing shoplifters for a living."

He was trying to make his way through chiropractic college and was just about out of money. Dolbin and his young wife were living in a $90-a-month apartment in downtown Chicago. "My son was born in the only bedroom in that apartment in downtown Chicago. He was born in that $90-a-month apartment because we couldn't afford to go to the hospital. I had no money to go back to school. My father died when I was 19. My family had no resources. I ended up in a quandary."

But nobody ever held onto a dream, or worked harder to make it real, than Jack Dolbin.

The World Football League had just started up, and it would be Dolbin's third attempt at a pro football career.

"The NFL was my fourth league," cracks Dolbin. "Pottstown was in the Continental League, the Coal Crackers were in the Seaboard Football League, and they were starting a team in Chicago in the World Football League."

A scout for the Chicago Fire had seen him play in college, knew he was living in Chicago, and knew he could run. Dolbin held all the Wake Forest records in the sprints, including the 100-yard and 220-yard dashes. Dolbin got a tryout in the bizarre netherworld of second-class football. "I didn't have contact lenses at the time, and I was wearing glasses. My wife loaned me her contact lenses, which were pretty close to my prescription."

He showed up at Soldier Field on a Saturday afternoon with about 300 other guys, went through some drills, and Dolbin ran a 4.3. "So automatically I caught some of their attention."

They invited about five of those 300 to camp in 1974, which turned out to be a strike year in the NFL. So lots of guys were drifting into the World Football League who had either been released or, given

JACK DOLBIN AT A GLANCE

POSITION: Wide Receiver
COLLEGE: Wake Forest University
PLAYING HEIGHT, WEIGHT: 5-10, 180
YEARS PLAYED FOR BRONCOS: 19754 979
UNIFORM NUMBER: 82
NOTABLE: Jack Dolbin was signed as a free agent by the Broncos in 1975 and played in every game until a serious knee injury ended his career in 1979. He was a starter at wide receiver for the Broncos in Super Bowl XII and averaged 16.7 yards per reception during his NFL career.
THE GAME: Kansas City at Denver, September 21, 1975

the strike, were looking for a place to play football. Thus creating even more competition for Dolbin just when he didn't need it.

Nobody ever said it was easy being Cinderella.

But beyond the injuries in college and the bad breaks that kept on coming, he had real talent to go along with perseverance for the ages. Dolbin played a year in the World Football League and led the team in receiving and touchdowns.

But his glory was short-lived. The Chicago Fire folded at the end of that season.

The Dolbin saga was reaching comical proportions. "Midway through the season we played in Hawaii, where I first met (future Broncos quarterback and teammate) Norris Weese. He was playing for the Hawaiians. They flew us over first class. They really did it right. It was very impressive the way they took care of us for what I think was the fourth game of the season. But by the 16th game of the season, they had already cancelled the last game of the season. We were down in Memphis, and our pregame meal was cold cheese sandwiches. We kind of got the idea that the league was in trouble."

When it folded—and few things have ever snapped shut as fast as the WFL did—Dolbin got about half of what he was supposed to have been paid. He had no place to go. He got his old job back chasing shoplifters at JC Penney.

But scouts had taken note of the WFL, and he finally started hearing from NFL teams.

And typical of the bizarre football world in which he lived, there is a story as to how Dolbin heard from the Broncos. "After leaving work at JC Penney's about 11 o'clock at night, the only thing open was the Pizza Palace. So I would always go by the Pizza Palace and get a slice, which I did that night. When I did, the fellow who owned the Pizza Palace, said, 'Your wife called. There's a fellow named John Ralston looking for you.'"

John Ralston was the general manager and head coach of the Denver Broncos. And he was calling a department store security guard to make him an offer.

From that moment on, it happened fast. The next morning he cut class, called the Broncos office, and listened to Ralston say those magic words: "We'd like to give you an opportunity to play in the National Football League."

That's all Dolbin needed to hear. "I would have signed for nothing." The Broncos gave him a check for $3,500 to sign, and a contract for $30,000. Dolbin remembers, "It seemed like it was from heaven."

Cinderella was moving to the Mile High City.

THE SETTING

The past events were surreal to the youthful receiver made grizzled by those five years, but they combined with his natural perspective to let him soak in every aspect of being a candidate for an NFL team.

He traveled to the team's rookie camp in May. "I'll never forget it because it was zero degrees." That is familiar to natives, as May weather in Denver is usually spectacular but subject to nature's whims.

Dolbin ran a 4.4 that day, plenty good enough to get their attention. And then he had shined for the rest of training camp, channeling all the talent, energy, and hope of a lifetime into the chance to make a dream come true.

Training camp was all the tougher because he was continually matched against Louis Wright, Denver's perennial all-pro cornerback. "In five years in the NFL playing against some of the best, nobody was as good as Louis Wright, and I had to go against him every day. So, just the fact that you can keep your confidence level up in that kind of situation is maybe worth mentioning. Louis was absolutely the best."

Going against Wright daily showed the coaches that the young veteran could line up at receiver in the NFL. And just as significant was the confidence it gave Dolbin, to whom life had already given numerous opportunities to believe he could not reach this goal.

But now the dream was coming true.

Training camp was held in Pomona, California, and when camp broke the team returned to Denver. "We were traveling on the plane back. The team hadn't had our first cut and was traveling 90 players, so we had to sit three across. I remember sitting between two veteran players who were complaining about having to sit three across. I had a flashback to those Pottstown days where we used to ride buses for 20 hours to play football. I was in the NFL. I hadn't yet played even an exhibition game, but I was traveling with the Denver Broncos."

The Broncos went through the six exhibition games, with Ralston putting together much of the talent that would be the make-up of the club which Red Miller drove to Super Bowl XII two years later. Dolbin spent weeks on the edge of his seat, but ultimately the Broncos cut two veteran receivers. The final roster included the young receiver from Pennsylvania's coal country, who finally would dress out in the NFL.

THE GAME OF MY LIFE

"When asked which game stands out most in my mind, it is easy to say the Super Bowl, or perhaps one of the playoff games against Oakland or Pittsburgh, but in all honesty it was my first NFL game. That game against Kansas City was the one," reflects Dolbin.

"A lot of things get the label 'unreal,' but this was truly was. Coming from the situation I came from, living in the $90-per-month apartment, and here I was two years later playing in the National Football League."

In the AFC West, down through the years, the rivalries always have been fierce, particularly among Denver, Kansas City, and Oakland. "It was a triad of rivalries," Dolbin says.

The first game of the season was against the Chiefs, a blood feud ever since the Chiefs began to call Kansas City their home following the 1962 season. And as with all things Bronco to this point in time, the Chiefs had bested the Broncos game after game, year after year, often times with embarrassment interjected into the ignominy of the final score itself.

But things were changing in Denver, with John Ralston's inspired player selection and veteran signal caller Charley Johnson showing the way to a talented young crew that did not know it was supposed to just roll over.

Dolbin remembers, "There was a lot of bitterness. It was in billboard material, locker-room material. There were game clippings up there, there were statements about various incidents, so a lot of the veterans were really getting into this. The rookies in the room were sensing that this game was a very important game."

The Broncos at that time were on the edge of being a playoff contender. They had only had two winning seasons, and they were the previous two years (7-52 in 1973 and 7-6-1 in 1974, both under Ralston).

The day was a long time coming for the young Dolbin. How many men would have abandoned the dream at a dozen logical places before forging this opportunity?

"Coming into Mile High Stadium, I remember driving back and parking in the players' lot. I went through my pregame activities, had my ankles taped, and my mind never drifted from the moment, and how it tied into all the moments that led me to this day.

"We came out to the field for opening day, and on the other sideline were the Kansas City Chiefs, and all that they stood for, in all of their glory."

Dolbin had won a share of a starting wide receiver position, alternating with Billy Van Heusen on the weak side. They actually brought in plays. Dolbin would play first and third downs and Van Heusen played second or vice versa, depending on how the plays fell.

Dolbin's ability to catch the ball was among the best of all receivers in Denver history; he was disciplined and tough. He was also on special teams for the Broncos, so the excitement level peaked with the opening kickoff, but that was hardly the end of the day. By day's end, Broncos fans would know Jack Dolbin.

Early in the first period, Johnson threw to Dolbin for the first time, but the ball was almost intercepted and fell harmlessly incomplete. In the second quarter, the Broncos recovered a Kansas City fumble at the Chiefs' 41-yard line, and on the second play after taking over, Johnson called Dolbin's number again.

The wide receiver remembers it still. "Charley called an 77-X-slant and that was me. It was a weak-side play. I ran a seven-yard inside slant. I remember coming out of the huddle, looking across the line of scrimmage, knowing that I was the primary receiver and the guy in front of me was Emmitt Thomas."

Thomas was a Pro Bowl cornerback for the Chiefs, and he had 58 career interceptions, so the challenge he presented was substantial. Dolbin recalls, "Then you had Willie Lanier in the middle of the field where I was supposed to run this pass pattern. So, I had to beat Emmitt Thomas who is covering me man for man and then somehow avoid Willie Lanier if I do catch the ball. Well, Willie blitzed, Emmitt laid off me about seven yards. If I couldn't do anything else, I could run. So I ran for a 39-yard touchdown."

Few players have ever matched talent with modesty as successfully as Dolbin, who could catch as well as he could run. And at just under

6 feet and 200 pounds, he had learned to use every nuance of his ability on the field.

The game teetered back and forth, and in the fourth quarter, Kansas City was holding a 33-24 lead. With under nine minutes left the Broncos drove from their 27 to the Chiefs 35. Running back Otis Armstrong took a handoff and went to the four-yard line before being hit by Thomas, who forced a fumble.

The crowd rose and moaned, but within a split second Dolbin, who had been downfield blocking on the play, picked up the loose ball and ran in for his second touchdown in the NFL.

"Otis ran a type of a draw play. I was driving my defender, Emmitt Thomas, downfield. When I saw Otis break through, I turned around and I hooked Emmitt and I was blocking him to the inside. Otis was running by me and he got hit by the safety and fumbled the ball at about the four-yard line. I was blocking Emmitt and I heard this commotion behind me, so I turned around and there was the ball on the ground. I just picked it up and dove into the end zone. I remember coming off the field after the game, and John Ralston came up to me and said, 'You know, a year ago Kansas City would have recovered that ball.' What he was saying was that the fact that I was downfield blocking, doing what I was supposed to do, I just happened to fall into it."

The Broncos scored once more, on a Johnson-to-Van Heusen pass that again burned Thomas, and Denver posted a dramatic 37-33 win over the archrival Chiefs.

Journey's end had come, and Jack Dolbin had arrived in the NFL.

He played five years for the Broncos, until a knee injury stopped his career for good, but those who watched him remember how he played the game.

"He was a model player," said Miller, his coach when Dolbin was a starter on Denver's 1977 Super Bowl team. "He was fast with superb

....

Receiver Jack Dolbin's first game with the Denver Broncos—September 21, 1975 against rival Kansas City—was the game of his life. He scored two touchdowns and the Broncos beat the Chiefs 37-33. *Courtesy of the Denver Broncos*

....

hands, technically proficient and had a very big heart. He was a pro's pro as a receiver."

AFTER THE CHEERING STOPPED

"I knew very early that you could only play so many years, and if injury didn't end your career, age would," says Dolbin. He had prepared to become a chiropractor, going back to school every off-season and finally finishing his education in 1978. "In fact, I used my Super Bowl bonus money to buy some equipment and open an office in north Denver. I practiced up there. Going into the '79 season, I would hire someone to come in and work the practice until the season was over, and then I would come in and take over. Actually, things worked out pretty well for me. I'm sure name recognition in the Denver area helped."

In addition to being a chiropractic physician, Dolbin owns a health club and is the director of a multidisciplinary health center in his native Pottsville.

After establishing a successful practice in the Denver area, Dolbin decided to return to his roots. "I loved Denver, but I didn't want to live in a big city, and Denver was a big city getting bigger. I wanted my kids to experience what I experienced growing up."

Dolbin's current home is in an economically depressed area. "The Pennsylvania coal region generally lags behind a bit, but it's a good area, with good people, great high school sports." The Dolbins moved back there in 1984 and he started his new practice, eventually expanding and ultimately starting a multidisciplinary practice. Dolbin hired an MD and a physical therapist, opened a health club, and never looked back.

He was on the medical staff at Villanova for 10 years from 1993 to 2003. "I would travel with the team and take care of their biomechanical injuries. I was responsible for about 500 scholarship athletes during that 10-year period. That really helped me stay involved in sports. I love the college atmosphere and I like working with young people."

Dolbin reflected on his vagabond journey in the world of pro football, with hopes and dreams as his steady companions.

"I have so many emotions relating back to all of my experiences in sports. Pottstown was, of course, a special experience. I can't tell you how great it was playing in Denver. I almost think it was divine guidance that led me to sign with Denver. I just felt such a comfort level with the Broncos. Everyone was very good to me. And I'm as proud of my Pottstown Firebirds championship ring as I am of my Super Bowl ring."

Chapter 15

STEVE ATWATER

BEFORE THE BRONCOS

Steve Atwater was one of the greatest defensive players in Denver Broncos history, a thunderous hitter from the beginning of his rookie year with the team.

Just as he was an immediate fixture in the Denver defensive backfield, football was a fixture in Atwater's life almost from the time he was old enough to know there was such a game.

"I started playing football when I was eight years old," he explains. "My dad took me out for a little league team and really didn't put any pressure on me. He just took me out to watch practice, which looked kind of exciting to me. And when we got home he said, 'Do you think you want to do that? You think you want to play football?' I said, 'Yeah, I think I could have fun at it.' So we went out the next day and got signed up."

It was a tough neighborhood, but family values and football would combine to lift young Steve above his circumstances to national athletic stardom.

Atwater took to the game immediately, and all of his early memories are good ones.

"I enjoyed the action and contact of the game right away. We had some really good teams back then. From when I was eight years old to when I was 13 years old, I don't remember losing more than two or three games. We had a lot of really good friends, a lot of good coaches. We just all played hard and had a lot of fun. The fun of the game is what it should be about for a youngster."

He was fortunate that his father was able to enroll him in a private Lutheran high school in St. Louis, where he received a quality education and earned a scholarship to play at the University of Arkansas.

Atwater always played with a sense of values and maturity. "I credit my upbringing at home and at school for that. My parents were great about it, and I was really lucky to get a strong value system early."

At the University of Arkansas he was a three-time All-Southwest Conference selection and a two-time All-American. "We had some success," Atwater notes modestly.

Then, as now, the Razorbacks were annual bowl participants, and Atwater was a legend by graduation. It was simply a matter of which pro team would use a first-round draft choice on the already-mature team leader.

"The Denver Broncos wound up drafting me with the 20th pick of the first round in 1989. Even though I knew I would be drafted high, I wouldn't have dreamed in a thousand years that I would go from where I came from to where I was: being picked in April of 1989 in the first round by an NFL team."

Drafted 20th overall in 1989 by the Broncos, Steve Atwater played in two Super Bowls that served as bookends to his career in Denver—Super Bowl XXIV in 1990 and Super Bowl XXXII in 1998. © *Eric Lars Bakke/Rich Clarkson and Associates*

THE SETTING

An immediate starter for the Broncos, Atwater and his teammates went to the Super Bowl in his 1989 rookie year, but suffered a crushing loss to the San Francisco 49ers.

"That was right at the end of the period when the team was going to the Super Bowl three times in four years, but after making it to the Super Bowl my first year, we were definitely demoralized in that game. It was embarrassing, the way we performed. We felt like we were much better, but for some reason couldn't get it together."

The Broncos were back in the AFC Championship game against Buffalo in 1991, but lost to the Bills. Atwater recalls, "My mind-set at that point was, 'Hey, every year or two we'll be in the AFC Championship game with a chance to get to the Super Bowl.' But of course it didn't happen that way. There were some coaching changes. It was not as easy to win as I had thought it would be."

Mike Shanahan came to the Broncos as head coach in 1995, with Atwater at that point firmly established as one of the game's best defensive players.

"When Mike came in, I felt that it was a different mind-set. He had a real emphasis on playing smart, playing hard, but he told us we were not going to necessarily beat each other up in practice and have all the physical challenges in practice, in terms of just tackling and similar drills. We were going to be fresh for the games. Our outlook was going to be bright, and we were going to be in a good state of mind, mentally. I've got to say, it worked."

The Broncos went 8-8 in Shanahan's first year. "It skyrocketed from there. I know it's all due to Mike Shanahan, his leadership, his organizational skills, the mind-set that he put into all of us that we could win, we could play with anybody, and we were champions. We all believed that. We all believed we were as good as anybody, and we believed we were prepared when we stepped on the field. We believed that we were fresher than they were. We believed that we were more physical than they were, and we believed we were smarter than they were.

STEVE ATWATER AT A GLANCE

POSITION: Safety
COLLEGE: University of Arkansas
PLAYING HEIGHT, WEIGHT: 6-3, 217
YEARS PLAYED FOR BRONCOS: 1989-98
UNIFORM NUMBER: 27
NOTABLE: A 2005 inductee into the Denver Broncos Ring of Fame, Steve Atwater was voted to a franchise-record seven consecutive Pro Bowls from 1990-96 and trails only John Elway (nine) for most Pro Bowl selections in team history. He was voted All-Pro by the Associated Press three times, 1991, 1992 and again in 1996.
THE GAME: Super Bowl XXXII, Green Bay vs. Denver, January 25, 1998, San Diego, California

"A lot of times in life—in football and in life—whatever you believe, that's really your reality. If you believe you're better than the other guy, you're going to play like it."

However, there was to be a real challenge associated with fulfilling that ultimate goal. In 1996, the Broncos had a great 13-3 record, best in the AFC, and were heavily favored as the playoffs began.

"But Jacksonville came in and upset us, and created this enormous emotional void that we had to fill. It was truly a crushing loss emotionally. A team could've done a lot of things, but we responded to what was a fantastic challenge, really, in that '97 season," Atwater explains.

"That was a big letdown because 1996 was really our first year of having that type of success. I think that we were a little bit shocked, but at the time we were feeling pretty good about ourselves in that we had the potential to go on and do some great things. And we get into the championship game against Jacksonville, and they basically came into our backyard and beat us up. I felt like we were prepared for the game. We certainly didn't come out and play as well as we could have played. But we rebounded from it that next year, and we said, 'Hey, you know, we see what we can do. We just have to make sure if we ever get in that position again that we cherish it and that we not take anything for granted and that we close on what we do, we finish it.' And we started getting that 'knockout-punch' attitude."

The Pro Bowl safety defers credit for that attitude to upper management. "That's a great testament to Mike Shanahan's leadership, all the other coaches, and Pat Bowlen just letting us know that, 'Hey guys, we had some success last year. We can do it. You've just got to believe, and we can do it. Put that out of your minds. You can use it for motivation if you want to, but it's a whole new year. Let's come back here, and let's win one ballgame at a time.'"

After entering the playoffs as a wild card, Atwater and the entire defense had terrific games, with wins at Kansas City and Pittsburgh setting up the Super Bowl XXXII contest against Green Bay in 1998.

"Even though we were a wild card, we felt like we were the better team. We felt like we were the best team in the NFL and that if we had a chance to, we would prove that and actually went into Kansas City. It was not an easy win. We all know Kansas City is one of the toughest stadiums to play in anyway. Pittsburgh also is a very tough environment for the visiting team.

"Once we won the conference with two road wins, we felt that the groundwork was laid and that we had already played our toughest two games in the toughest two places. After all, we had won at KC and Pittsburgh, and we got to play the Packers in a neutral site, which also happened to be an AFC West city and stadium that we played in every year. We felt very, very comfortable going into San Diego for that game."

THE GAME OF MY LIFE

"So we were way down in the odds—big underdogs. Then, the Green Bay guys, they start talking noise! They were putting fuel on the fire all week long, so we just said, 'OK, we've got to sit back and kind of bite our tongues. We don't want to get into a verbal war with them and give them anything to get fired up about.' We just kind of laid back and let that frustration and that anger build. Come game day, I felt like we exploded, and we unleashed it. Everybody on that Bronco team came to play.

"During the week we took a very humble approach and laid in the weeds. But the Packers, I think that they thought that they had it all set up for them. They didn't know what was coming their way Sunday.

"We would compliment their receivers and their running backs. We remember saying how we didn't know how we were going to stop them, and they were like, 'Yeah, you're right. I don't know how they're going to stop us.' It really kind of ticked us off. You would think they would say, 'Hey, you know, they've got a good defense. They've got a good offense. It's going to be a good game.' But it wasn't like that. They said, 'Hey, we're the better team. We're going to run over them. We're going to catch passes here and there.' It was kind of a surprise to see that in such a big game. In our opinion, we didn't think that they respected us."

On Super Bowl Sunday, Steve Atwater had arguably the greatest game by a safety, in the greatest game in the history of the franchise. He had six tackles, all first-hit tackles. He had a sack, forced a fumble, knocked down two passes, and was a devastating physical presence all day long.

"On their first third-down play of the game we kept our regular defense in. They had three wide receivers in. Antonio Freeman ran a post route, and they had the outside receivers running go routes. I hit Antonio Freeman coming across the middle. They got the first down but I got a pretty good hit on him. And then they went down, and they scored on the drive. We had to slow them down just a little bit, get our bearings. We did that."

Green Bay had 76 yards on the opening drive of the game, but the high-powered Green Bay offense commanded by Brett Favre managed just 274 yards in the remaining 56 minutes.

"We tried to give them a different look and hoped we could confuse them some. Green Bay was a very physical team, and we knew it would be physical all day long," Atwater recalls.

He was at or near the scene of the tackle all day long. After the Broncos tied it up at 7-7, Atwater blitzed Favre on Green Bay's next

Steve Atwater celebrates after sacking Packers quarterback Brett Favre (4), causing him to fumble in the second quarter of Super Bowl XXXII, the game of Atwater's life. © David Gonzales/Rich Clarkson and Associates

possession, forcing a hurried throw. Tyrone Braxton picked off the pass, setting up the Broncos' second touchdown drive of the day.

In the second quarter, Atwater sacked the Green Bay quarterback, forcing a fumble. The Broncos recovered to set up a Jason Elam field goal that put Denver on top by a 10-point margin. Regarding his forced fumble against Favre, Atwater recalls, "It was just a blitz. No one picked me up on that play. I was supposed to do that on that play."

In this game, the leading Denver tacklers were Atwater, Braxton, cornerback Ray Crockett, and linebacker John Mobley, each with six. Three of those players were defensive backs, and that was not unnoticed by Atwater. "They probably thought we (the defensive backs) were the weakness, so they threw quite a few passes on us. We really thought they were going to come out and try and run the ball more than they did. But they wanted to pass. I'm sure that with Brett being the great quarterback that he was, they wanted to give him the greatest chance to win the ballgame. But, personally for us, we came to play."

One of the passes that Atwater knocked down was at the end of a spectacular dash to the sideline to get to the ball. So critical is Atwater of himself, he recalls the play thusly: "I remember dropping that interception that could've helped us in that victory. I was heading out of bounds at full speed when I touched it, but it was one that I should've had. We had a blitz on. I was covering man-to-man. We had that same blitz on earlier, and they completed the pass to Freeman running a deep inside route. We figured they would try to come back to that play. I'm sure (receiver Robert) Brooks thought he was open, but I was able to get a good drive on it and knock it down. That's one that I wish I had, but you never know. If I'd have gotten the interception, maybe something else would have been different. So I'm glad that it turned out exactly the way it did."

The Broncos held the Packers under 100 yards rushing for the game, and late in the contest Denver was holding onto its 31-24 lead as Favre marched his team down the field on what everyone knew was the Packers' final drive.

"That last drive was a great challenge for us. People had not given our defense a lot of credit, and I would not have wanted it any other way than having to stop them at the end. It was our job to keep them out of the end zone."

A day of huge hits by Atwater—always known as one of the game's most powerful safeties—almost ended in disaster for the Broncos.

"It was third down and long, and Favre threw the ball up to the middle of the field. I just remember breaking on the ball, saying, 'I cannot let anybody touch this ball.' I remember hitting (Denver defensive back) Randy Hilliard and also (Green Bay receiver) Robert Brooks, and next thing I remember is sitting there talking to Greek (trainer Steve Antonopulos)."

He had knocked himself, Hilliard, and Brooks out of the game, putting Denver two men down in the secondary against Brett Favre.

"I definitely didn't want to miss that last play of the game, but I had no choice. I was knocking some cobwebs out of my head. On the last play for the Packers—fourth and six—we called a blitz and got some pressure on Brett. He threw it, and I remember John Mobley knocking the ball down. Like I said, I still had some cobwebs, so I don't recall thinking, 'OK, if we stop these guys, we win the game.' Never did that cross my mind. So when Mobley knocked the ball down, I just happened to glance up at the scoreboard, and I said, 'Hey, this is over, we win! We're the champs!' And all of a sudden, it hit me! And even now when I talk about it, I get chill bumps because that play—John Mobley knocking that ball down, me looking up and seeing the clock and realizing we won—that was the most fabulous moment I had as an NFL player.

"So many thoughts raced through my head. Individual honors are good, but they do not complete you. You're not really complete until you win the big game with your team. Football is a team sport that, from the time you start to the day you finish, you can't play by yourself. To be able to put it together, aside from all the injuries, all the other distractions, to be able to put it together and win an NFL championship is a huge feat. We were able to do that. And, like I said, we had some disappointments the year before, losing to Jacksonville. We hadn't been to the AFC Championship game since 1991. It was just a long time coming, and that was my eighth season. I cherished it. I said, 'Hey, we accomplished something great. It took eight years to get to this point, and it may not come again for a while. Just realize how special this moment is and cherish it and know what it took to get here.' It took a lot of hard work, a lot of sacrifice, and a lot of guys putting their egos aside to play together and listen to our coaches and not bicker.

"We felt like it was a piano that just slid off our backs. The AFC is back. The city of Denver, having lost the other four Super Bowls they had gone to. I felt really good for the fans all across the country because you know, Bronco fans are all over the place. But especially the fans there in Denver who sit through all the games in the cold, the heat, the rain. For them to be with us and experience that, I felt really good for them to be able to go to work and say, 'My team won the Super Bowl. We're champs.' The team, the fans, we were all champs at last."

AFTER THE CHEERING STOPPED

Steve Atwater was always comfortable with his life and his life preparation. During the players' lunch break he could be seen at his locker reading a book about money management or real estate. So it was no surprise when he dived into that field full time.

"I always had a lot of interest in how finance works, so this was a natural progression for me," he explains. "I invest in real estate, mostly commercial, also apartments, some retail centers. I also own an online travel agency, atwaterworldtravel.com."

He and wife Letha have four children, and the proud father likes to focus his interest on family. "We have three boys and a girl. The boys, Stephen, Di Andre, and Paris, are all real good students, love sports and are real good athletes. Then our little girl, Malaysia, she's five, is taking some acting classes and ballet. She's my little sweetheart. You've always got to have one of those that bring you back down to earth."

The Atwater family moved to the Atlanta area after his retirement from football and he notes that the climate is such that he can still squeeze in some golf, in between following the activities of his children and managing his diversified business interests.

Broncos fans always placed Atwater in elite status among his teammates. He was a special member of the Denver franchise.

This humbles Atwater. "I am so grateful to the Broncos organization for everything. First off, for having the confidence in me to select me in the first round, because you never know what you're getting with a guy. You hope that you've done your research and it's going to pay off, but you never know what you're getting. I've always been thankful that they drafted me.

"Everything just seemed to align perfectly in Denver, as far as I was concerned. I had a great relationship with Mr. Bowlen throughout my career, and I'm deeply gratified.

"I have a great deal of gratitude and thanks that I was made so welcome into the Bronco family.

"And as to being inducted into the Ring of Fame, Denver is in my Ring of Fame. I just have a special place in my heart. To be honored by the team that has really put me on the map and provided many years of wonderful times, many lifelong friendships, I don't even know how I could thank the organization and Mr. Bowlen, Mike Shanahan, (former coach) Dan Reeves, and (former general manager) John Beake.

"When I was playing, I enjoyed that. In retirement, you move on to other aspects of your life, and your focus goes elsewhere. But to know that my name will be on the façade of the stadium forever as one of the team's most honored players, that will always mean a great deal to me.

"I don't know how I could thank everyone for what they gave me."

How he thanked everyone was simply by doing what they asked him to do. He not only played great, which is beyond what one can ask, but he was a leader and captain.

Atwater exemplified character. He was the epitome of what one hopes a player can be. Every class needs a student body president, and Atwater more than adequately filled that role.

Chapter 16

JIM TURNER

BEFORE THE BRONCOS

Jim Turner grew up in a small working-class town in northern California, feisty and competitive and chippy. He had to be in his neighborhood, where you pushed back when you got pushed. It made him very competitive, and like most kids he played all the high school sports.

But Turner played them like he had something to prove, like he had someplace to go, becoming a high school All-American before setting off to Utah State as a quarterback and placekicker.

Back in the era before cable TV had games on seemingly every night, from every conference, Utah State and Jim Turner played in the relative wide-open spaces and anonymity of the American West. He was a straight-on kicker, not soccer-style, and eventually would be recognized as the last guy in football wearing black high tops when literally every other player in the game was wearing more stylish footwear.

But Jim Turner was born old school, and has it tattooed on his psyche for all to see, if not embrace.

In his senior year the Aggies played in a New York bowl game at the legendary Polo Grounds. "It was the dreaded Gotham Bowl, which I believe to this day is the only postseason bowl game ever played in New York City. There must have been 1,800 pigeons, and no people there," Turner remembers. But among the few in attendance were pro football scouts.

A side benefit to that appearance at the Polo Grounds was that the fledgling American Football League New York team got a peek at him, and one year later in 1964, he was a rookie with the Jets.

Preparation, work ethic, and a fierce competitive spirit met timing, and Turner entered pro football as it began its explosion into the American social fabric.

Ultimately, the Western-born Turner kicked for seven years in New York, making his mark by leading the league in extra-point percentage in five of those years, and leading pro football in both points scored and field goals made in both 1968 and 1969.

He played in the first football game at Shea Stadium, an easy 30-6 Jets win over the Denver Broncos in what was also the first game of his career, opening day 1964. "The farthest thoughts from my mind that night were that I would kick 16 years in pro football, and that I would ever be back out West playing for the Broncos."

He also played in the very first game of *Monday Night Football*, well before it too became ingrained in the weekly TV schedule of every household.

"We walked into that game thinking one thing: 'Who was the fool that brought up kicking off at this outrageous time of the night?' Of course it became the greatest thing going. We felt we were just going to just walk away with that game over Cleveland, and I missed a field goal that night and they beat us."

Kicker Jim Turner retired with the second-most field goals in NFL history with 304, including a game-winner with three seconds left against Oakland in the game of his life on October 22, 1973. *Rod Hanna/Denver Broncos*

Turner was getting used to his place on the national stage, and he cemented his reputation as one of the game's great clutch kickers in Super Bowl III, with three critical high-pressure field goals in the Jets' 16-7 upset win over the Baltimore Colts. Joe Namath had guaranteed that win, but New York could not have pulled it off without Turner's three-for-three performance in front of what at the time was the greatest television audience ever to watch a pro football game.

In 1970, he was traded to the Broncos, where he would play for nine more years and help lead Denver to its first Super Bowl appearance following the 1977 season.

"I think kicking in Shea Stadium prior to becoming a Denver Bronco would harden anybody," Turner says philosophically. "New York is hard to play in. The winds at Shea were brutal, and coming from a town of only 1,800 to growing up with the Jets and in New York, I was ready when I came to Denver."

There was not much to the Broncos team that Turner joined in 1971. The Broncos had been absolute and perpetual losers, poster children for defeatism.

THE SETTING

"The stage was being set by the time I got to Denver. I came to a team in Denver just like a team that I had gone to with the Jets—very young, very disorganized and not very good. When I got to Denver, Denver was not a very good team—it really wasn't. But John Ralston (head coach and general manager of the Broncos) and Carroll Hardy (player personnel director) were putting together, personnel wise, a pretty outstanding group of men through trades, drafts, and the whole bit. You could see the organization grow, and over the next couple of years we began to feel we could play with anybody," Turner notes.

But while Denver was on the cusp of success, the Broncos and the Mile High City in 1973 were still languishing on the national stage. And in pro football, nothing defined the national stage like Monday night, where the Broncos had no presence whatsoever. Broncos fans perceived the situation as one in which they, their town, and their

JIM TURNER AT A GLANCE

POSITION: Kicker
COLLEGE: Utah State University
PLAYING HEIGHT, WEIGHT: 6-2, 205
YEARS PLAYED FOR BRONCOS: 1971-1979
UNIFORM NUMBER: 15
NOTABLE: A 1988 inductee into the Denver Broncos Ring of Fame, Jim Turner retired second in NFL history in career scoring (1,439 points) and second in field goals (304). He was just the fourth player to kick 500 extra points (521 total).
THE GAME: Oakland at Denver, October 22, 1973

team got zero national respect, and they were not far wrong in that assessment.

Monday Night Football in its early stages was all about Howard Cosell. Turner, the veteran of seven years in New York, recalls, "The circus was coming to town, and an old friend of mine was leading the parade into the city. I loved Howard Cosell. I knew him from my Jet days. He was at practice every day in New York, doing his radio interviews with that bulky, primitive old equipment, before football on Monday was even a concept.

"But when he came to town he didn't have much respect for a town he probably had never been in, looking at Denver as a hick cow town in the sparsely populated Rocky Mountain time zone."

Indeed, *Monday Night Football* was all about huge audience numbers, and the Broncos played in America's Forgotten Time Zone in terms of national TV watchers. Don Meredith was "Dandy Don," Frank Gifford was trying to hold it together, and collectively they didn't know much, or care much, about the Denver Broncos. "And we're playing the dreaded Oakland Raiders, which every football fan in American knew about, with the very colorful John Madden as the coach," Turner explains.

The Broncos had started the 1973 season 2-3, but as Turner recalls, "We were just getting better every practice. Not every game, every practice. The team was getting more confident, and we just knew that we could play with anybody. And then there was the excitement of being in Denver's first Monday night game, where the fans are going crazy. They had seen these games on Monday night and now they were going to be a part of it. They were painting their homes orange, their cars orange, and it was outrageously fun.

"We were ready."

So *Monday Night Football* was in Denver, but the game was not about the Broncos, until they made it so.

THE GAME OF MY LIFE

Leading up to that *Monday Night Football* game, the Broncos were a team that had never had a winning season, which was contrary to what Turner had had in his own career.

No kicker ever took more pride in his pregame preparation than Turner. "My routine prior to a game, and I learned this from (Jets coach) Weeb Eubank, was rather simple. You had to know where the wind was. You had to know which way it was blowing so you could help the coach on the opening kickoff and you had to be ready to kick from anywhere within range, regardless of angle. And I always made sure that I knew where a certain flag was or a piece of string on the netting. I knew where everything was in the stadium. It was our stadium. Not only would I work on various kicks that kickers work on during pregame, but I had a purpose to a lot of them. I'd get out there, put it up in the air and just kind of see if it would blow out or not. We had a book on every stadium, and I certainly had a book on Mile High."

Late in the first quarter Denver struck first, with safety Billy Thompson picking up an Oakland fumble deep in Bronco territory and rambling untouched for an 80-yard touchdown.

The Raiders answered back in the second quarter. First with a 35-yard field goal by the ageless George Blanda, then with an 80-yard strike from Ken Stabler to wide receiver Mike Siani, closing out a dominant period with a long drive to the Denver six. The Broncos held and forced Oakland to settle for another Blanda field goal, this one from 13 yards out to give Oakland a 13-7 halftime lead.

The memory of that night remains vivid for Turner. "I always felt that George Blanda was one of the toughest competitors ever. As a clutch quarterback and clutch kicker, he stared down a lot of big moments, and in the first half, I just had the feeling that it was going to come down to a kicking contest between George and myself."

The Broncos stubbornly fought back in the third quarter, taking six minutes to drive down for a one-yard touchdown by Floyd Little. On the ensuing drive, Denver forced and recovered a fumble at the Oakland 43; but the Broncos' drive stalled, and Turner went out to kick a 43-yard field goal.

Turner's thoughts of the kicking contest between two old pros were beginning to play themselves out in reality. Denver led, 17-14, with Charley Johnson leading the two scoring drives for the Broncos.

"We had some real veteran leadership, and our team was not just going to roll over. Charlie Johnson was a terrific quarterback, a brilliant guy. His arm was gone, with all of the shoulder surgeries, and he'd been banged around a lot with Houston and the old St. Louis Cardinals, but he was exactly what that team needed at that time with their growth and development—a solid veteran quarterback who knew the game inside and out, a good teammate. There was no fooling around. The fact that he went out there and played hurt a lot really made an impact on the young players, and the Raiders were banging him around every chance they could.

"That night against the Raiders, at that time of our puberty, if you will, we needed him."

After Denver took the lead, Oakland had a workman-like drive that took up the rest of the third quarter, with Stabler passing 16 yards to Cliff Branch to make it 20-17 as the fourth quarter began.

And from there, the old pros took over the night.

Denver drove from its own 13 to a fourth down at the Oakland 30, where Turner came out, measured it off, and planted a 37-yard field goal to knot the game at 20.

It was a stirring night at Mile High Stadium, the highest degree of attention and drama focused on a Denver sporting event.

The teams exchanged punts until the Raiders began a drive with 3:32 left. Every spectator was aware of Blanda's proclivity for late-game heroics.

As if written in a script, Oakland methodically moved and held the ball until just 36 seconds remained in the game, when Blanda calmly went out to kick a 49-yard field goal to put the Raiders ahead, 23-20, seemingly for the duration.

But kicking was a huge part of that game, and those final 36 seconds included not one, but three more kicks.

Turner explains how those final 36 seconds unfolded, "After they scored, Ray Guy kicked off for them, but he twice kicked balls out of bounds. He kicked off for George and he kicked two balls out of bounds. He gave us great field position, and Charley Johnson came over to me before we started that last drive down, which took all but the final three seconds and he said, 'Lace 'em up, we're going for the field goal.' We marched right down, a pass to Floyd for 13, a draw play to Joe Dawkins for 12, and then Floyd to the right side of the line for nine more. All the while, the fans were going nuts, and the Raiders were in shock."

That left just three seconds on the clock. Time enough for Turner to take his black high tops onto the turf for one more time, his third field-goal attempt of the night.

There was no overtime in those days, so a tie would be as good as a win for the longest suffering fans in pro football, and for a franchise trying to find itself.

Turner measured it and calmly set himself as the clock ran down. "I was lucky enough to make the field goal," he says, although when you make 304 field goals in the NFL, preparation trumps luck in the description of how it happens.

The reality is that Turner was a tough, hardened guy, absolutely confident every time he left the sideline to ply his trade.

"I liked those kinds of kicks. I think kickers are a different breed. I think they are very tough minded. You can call it cocky if you want, but you've got to be tough minded like a relief pitcher or a goalie in hockey. You've got to forget that last one, you've got to go out there and do it, and for some reason I really liked kicking on the same field as George Blanda and Jan Stenerud. My respect was deep for them and I thought to myself, 'This little boy from Crockett is as good as them in crunch time.' And I just really enjoyed it."

Turner's third field goal of the night, as time and the telecast expired, secured itself a place in Broncos lore. "It was a fantastic night and a great win for the city."

He was a tough-minded, old-school guy and this was hardly the only big game Turner ever had in an illustrious 16-year pro career, but once again his timing was fantastic for an entire franchise.

"Broncos fans everywhere knew that in order to get good you had to be able to compete with the Raiders. You could beat San Diego, you could match up with Kansas City, but even though they were good, the Raiders were always the yardstick. Whether it was because nobody liked them, whether it was because John Madden was 'the fat man,' whether people didn't like Al Davis, whatever. They were the yardstick, and once we were able to play them nose to nose, then the guys knew, the page had been turned and let's go forward."

The fans, networks, and national media knew it too. As a city, Denver did not occupy the same place on the national stage as it had going in. "The whole thing picked up momentum," Turner recalls. "Denver was not just a dustbowl place in the middle of the mountains, but a real place, with a real team that needed to be accounted for.

"The next morning I was on the radio in New York with Dick Schaap and everybody was saying, 'Gee, I didn't know you guys could play that good of football.' They discovered this dusty little cow town, and I am so proud to have been a part of it."

AFTER THE CHEERING STOPPED

Jim Turner finished his illustrious football career and dabbled in broadcasting for a time, doing some radio as well as a stint doing the color on NFL games for NBC. But mostly, he settled into retirement, which proved hard for a guy like Turner. He just had to be doing something.

The "something" turned out to be the rebirth of Jim Turner.

He became involved in a program put together with the support of the National Football Foundation, which is the amateur arm of high school and college football. "Everything is student-athlete, student first," says Turner. "The program that I am involved in is called Play it Smart. Jefferson Senior High School was about the fifth school in America and I took over Alameda High School, too, because I absolutely love working with these young, mostly minority, at-risk kids.

"The kids remind me of myself growing up in a small town called Crockett, California. A tough town, and tough times, and anything I can do to tutor and mentor these kids, I will do."

And he has done enough to be written up in numerous publications, including an article in *Sports Illustrated* about Turner and the dramatic success of the program.

"I love being with these young people. They are exciting. We've got good things happening. I have over 70 in college right now, in the last six years. I've got some college graduates now. A couple of my kids I'm worried about, because they are in Iraq. We've got honor-roll students. I'm their tutor, they have to spend an hour a day with me," Turner says, noting that it is not possible for them to put much past him in the way of excuses.

"I tell them, 'Fellas, I wrote the book.'"

During the football season he spends time daily on the field with his kids. "I really try and stay out of the coaches' way but when it comes to the kicking game and kickers and punters, I have a little bit of input there. I love to work with those kids."

Turner takes obvious pride and gratification in the program. "I honestly thought I would just be raising my flowers in the garden and raising the grandkids."

Broncos owner Pat Bowlen has been personally and financially supportive of Turner and the Play it Smart program, and Turner notes that the involved kids have benefited tremendously.

Pat Bowlen and his Ring of Fame committee voted Turner into that façade of honor in 1988. Turner recalls, "I was doing radio up at training camp in Greeley. [Bowlen] came into our media trailer there and told me that I had been selected, and I actually teared up because

I'm thinking, 'Wow, a special teams guy, a placekicker.' And I wasn't always the most popular guy because I took some hard stands in my time. I wear that ring proudly. I don't wear my Super Bowl ring often but I wear that Broncos ring. You have to understand my total background and how big of a deal that was and what it is like to walk into the stadium and see my name up there."

So it went full circle for Jim Turner, from growing up in a working-class town to being immortalized in the team's Ring of Fame.

"Coming from a small high school like I did, to retiring as the second leading scorer in history of the game, it's all amazing to me still.

"It tickled me to be put under gun. It always has, and that's the only damn thing I miss!"

Chapter 17

KARL MECKLENBURG

BEFORE THE BRONCOS

Karl Mecklenburg is the son of a doctor father and a mother who worked in foreign diplomacy, but he grew up like any other kid who liked to get dirty. In fact, as a player he often said, "I'm a lousy football watcher; I like to play."

He was known as "Meck" just as easily as Karl, and was a tough, competitive kid from the start of little league.

He came to the Broncos as a 12th-round draft choice. "I wasn't a great athlete as a kid. As a ninth grader I was the smallest starter on our football team. As a junior in high school I played JV football. I didn't even make the varsity team."

But he loved getting dirty and would never give it up. Mecklenburg had lots of college options as a student, but chose instead to enroll at tiny Augustana College on a one-third scholarship with the understanding that if he played well he would get a full scholarship.

After his second year there the coach called Mecklenburg into the office. He had led the team in sacks that year, playing every down on defense, so the young lineman felt good about things, but that optimism was squashed quickly. "Coach called me in and told me that he knew my dad was a doctor and that he could afford this school and that they were taking away my scholarship and bringing someone else in."

Naturally, the coach hoped Meck would sign off on that plan. Instead he signed up as a walk-on at Minnesota. But NCAA rules dictate that when a player transfers between four-year colleges, he has to sit out for a year. Mecklenburg laughs as he remembers, "When you sit out, you're basically a scout-team player. So I was sweeping up the weight room if I wanted to be at the training table."

But he was a good enough practice-squad player that when he was eligible for a scholarship, they gave him one.

Just a week later in the spring game he tore a ligament in his knee and they tried to have him give the scholarship back. "They wouldn't let me rehab my knee in the men's training room so I had to go to the women's training room to rehab my knee," he recalls. "It was really a tough situation, but through it all I always really loved to play football. And I learned that even if things aren't always going right you can fight through it, and if you work hard enough you can be successful."

Everything worked out in Mecklenburg's favor, and not just because he was one of the few male Gopher athletes rehabbing in the women's training room. He survived that situation, and the next year led the Big 10 in sacks. "After that there was no question about whether or not I deserved the scholarship."

The football world is small, he explains. "One of the amazing things about my University of Minnesota experience is that Mike Shanahan was there when I got there. Tony Dungy was a graduate assistant, who I worked with as a scout-team player and Mike Martz

---

Karl Mecklenburg was drafted by the Broncos in the 12th round, and he played his entire 12-year career—including three Super Bowls—in orange and blue.
Courtesy of the Denver Broncos

was in the film room. We had pretty good coaching when I was there." All three ended up in the NFL, with Shanahan's glittering Broncos career overlapping Mecklenburg's.

THE SETTING

The Broncos drafted Mecklenburg in the 12th round, having scored very high on the NFL's rookie player intelligence test and demonstrated versatility on defense against tough Big 10 competition.

He came to a rookie camp like no other in Denver history.

John Elway, the most ballyhooed prospect since Joe Namath, was turning heads and commanding all the media's attention. "All eyes were on John, so the rest of us came in under the radar, which kind of let me and some other rookies just concentrate on football."

Plus, Meck was about as unheralded as any player could be. All the rookies were brought out to meet the Denver press and get some publicity. Mecklenburg stood out in the way that no PR man ever desires: Not a single journalist asked him a question. Mecklenburg, it turns out, was not bothered by it, saying, "It was a strange time. John had attracted so much attention at that time that I didn't feel bad or hurt."

It's a long road from being ignored by the press to being named to the Denver Broncos Ring of Fame, but Meck covered that ground very fast.

It was very early in camp when the young blond from Minnesota made his mark. Broncos coach Dan Reeves was trying to put in his offense, lining them up and running plays against the very end of the defensive depth chart, which included Mecklenburg—except Mecklenburg was playing like a guy who wouldn't be spending very long at that end of the rotation.

After three or four straight plays in which Mecklenburg seemed to reach the quarterback with ease, Reeves called defensive coordinator Joe Collier over and joked, "Can you do something about that kid? I'm trying to put my offense in, and every play he keeps coming in touching the quarterback like 'Tag, you're it.'"

KARL MECKLENBURG AT A GLANCE

POSITION: Linebacker
COLLEGE: University of Minnesota
PLAYING HEIGHT, WEIGHT: 6-3, 240
YEARS PLAYED FOR BRONCOS: 1983-1994
NOTABLE: Inducted into the Denver Broncos Ring of Fame in 2001, Karl Mecklenburg established himself as one of the greatest defensive players in franchise history during his 12-year career. Mecklenburg was voted into six Pro Bowls (1985-87, 1989, 1991, and 1993). He was named All-AFC and All-NFL four times (1985-87 and 1989). Named AFC Player of the Year by Football News in 1986, Mecklenburg played in three Super Bowls (XXI, XXII, and XXIV). He is second in team history with 79.5 sacks, with his career-high 13 occurring in 1985. Mecklenburg had 11 multi-sack games and is the only player in Broncos history to record four sacks in a game twice in a career. He was inducted into the Colorado Sports Hall of Fame in 2001.
THE GAME: Denver at Pittsburgh, December 1, 1985

The idea being that the defense wasn't supposed to be doing well against those guys at that moment. "Yeah, I had a pretty good camp," Mecklenburg acknowledges. "I actually had to go and find somebody to be my agent when I got drafted. It wasn't like I had agents banging on my door.

"That was nothing new for me. I had always had things which I had overcome in the past, and I'd expected to overcome things again at that point."

He channeled all his talent into becoming a terrific pro player, and rapidly became a fan favorite. But going into his third season, he still was not well known on a national level.

His breakout year was 1985. He would go on to make the Pro Bowl that year, after setting a new Broncos record with 13 quarterback sacks. He made virtually every national All-NFL team that year, with his versatility enabling the coaching staff to move him around considerably in the Denver defense.

He was so versatile, in fact, that despite the spectacular season he was having, Mecklenburg did not become a full-time starter until week 10 of the season.

And three weeks later, the Broncos played the Steelers in Pittsburgh.

THE GAME OF MY LIFE

It was December 1, 1985, the Broncos were playing at Pittsburgh against a team that was always a load.

That Denver won the game by a 31-23 score took a back seat to the play of Karl Mecklenburg. He lined up at all seven down positions that day and wreaked havoc all over the Pittsburgh backfield.

"That was the first time that Joe Collier and (linebackers coach) Myrel Moore decided to see if I could play different positions. I had moved around a little bit from position to position as a matter of course for them to try to find a place where I fit, but this was really the first time that they had really moved me around inside the game. They moved me around into several positions to try and make some match-up problems for the Steelers."

Mecklenburg had six tackles and knocked down a pass in that game against the Steelers, but it was his amazing presence from seven defensive positions that stunned onlookers. His ferocious pass rush produced a Broncos team-record four sacks. (He would have four sacks in one other game that season—no other Denver player has ever had that single-game total twice in a season.) Beyond even the sacks, he seemed to be in the Pittsburgh backfield all afternoon.

He had two sacks in the second quarter to thwart Pittsburgh drives, forcing the Steelers to settle for two field goals that produced a 10-6 Denver lead at halftime. Both of those sacks forced Steelers fumbles, and even though Pittsburgh recovered both, the tone was set.

"It was amazing the way it worked out. I did not know what I was doing in a lot of the situations. I was playing outside linebacker and trying to remember what my reads were, and eventually it just came down to getting the guy with the ball. I just fell back on that, and it was amazing; everything worked out well."

In the third quarter Mecklenburg put an end to two Pittsburgh drives with third-down sacks of quarterback David Woodley, who went down six times overall at the hands of Broncos defenders.

Mecklenburg was always better at playing than performing drill work, and the higher the stakes, the bigger his presence seemed to be. A road game against a tough opponent is about as daunting as it can get in the NFL.

The Ring of Fame pass rusher thinks a lot of it is mental. "There is a mind-set that a player can get in when things are going well, like they did in that game. They call it 'the zone' or other things, but time slows down and you do things that you couldn't do otherwise, and I was in the zone a lot that day."

He was still in that zone in the fourth quarter, when Denver was holding a 24-23 lead with under two minutes to play. Pittsburgh had driven to its own 41 when Woodley was feeling the final pressure of the day by Mecklenburg and threw a pass that was intercepted and returned 41 yards for the decisive score by Bronco cornerback Mike Harden.

The Broncos had a win at Pittsburgh, and Karl Mecklenburg had a reputation that had spread from one time zone to four.

"I remember one particular play where I was playing outside linebacker on the right side. It was a sweep play on which the fullback was supposed to block me. I remember looking at a guy who was lying on the ground—he was trying to cut block me. Slow motion kind of set in for me, and I just stepped around him and tackled the running back like it was nothing. And then on Monday, watching it on tape at normal speed and it was like, 'Wow! I did that.'"

Generally in a passing situation Joe Collier would put Meclklenburg at right defensive end. But Mecklenburg recalls, "In the Pittsburgh game I was moving around a lot, more than ever before,

and the sacks came from both the inside linebacker and defensive end positions."

That was not the extent of his mobility against the Steelers. The Broncos also had a three-defensive-linemen package in which Mecklenburg would play over the nose on pass-rushing situations. He also saw action at both outside linebacker spots.

"When I was playing outside linebacker, what we were trying to do was draw attention outside of the field and bring somebody from the other side a lot of the time.

"Things really came together that day. I had been given a great opportunity. Basically, the coaches said, 'We are going to call the game in a way that puts you at the point of attack, or at least where we think the point of attack needs to be.' Wherever the Steelers were running, the Broncos coaches would switch me to that position," he says, crediting his defensive teammates for their adjustments that day as well.

"The other guys all had to move around, which is a great testament to the other guys. They all had to learn more than one position for that game, too."

Among the press box attendees was veteran football writer Paul Zimmerman of *Sports Illustrated*. Zimmerman was far and away recognized as one of America's leading authorities within the sportswriting fraternity, and his story in that week's issue singled out Mecklenburg's performance as the key to Denver's win.

His career took on a national scope from that time forward, and Mecklenburg's career ended with him being selected for the Denver Broncos Ring of Fame, as well as receiving annual candidacy for the Pro Football Hall of Fame.

Linebacker Karl Mecklenburg's game of his life was played against Pittsburgh on December 1, 1985, when he lined up at all seven down positions, notching six tackles and four sacks.
Dee Welsch/Denver Broncos

AFTER THE CHEERING STOPPED

By the time Mecklenburg stopped playing, his family was settled in Denver, finding a great match in climate, lifestyle, and comfort level.

"I took a lot from pro football for my future—the challenges of preparation, playing injured, going beyond where you thought you could go or where anyone else thought you could go, physically, mentally, and emotionally."

Wise with his money and armed with the knowledge that you can't play forever, he now runs his own motivational speaking business and finds that there are challenges very similar to those of football.

His talks focus on several themes: "teamwork, courage, dedication, constant learning and refusing to quit."

Mecklenburg has a number of corporate clients for his speeches, and in addition serves as a spokesman for a couple of local firms.

"The thing I miss the most about football is the adrenaline rush that the competition provides, and I had to learn how to transfer that to the motivational speaking world. Once I did, it was a tremendous help to me," he says.

Instead of rushing the passer before 75,000 screaming fans, Mecklenburg now meets the public 500 to 1,000 at a time. "I'm getting the same rush from this as I did before a game against the Raiders. I love it. Some guys bungee jump, some guys drive too fast, I get up in front of people and speak."

He notes that his fame has been a big help in developing the new business, but the softspoken Ring of Famer says some of his best friends now are guys that he played ball with and against in a Denver uniform.

Few players were as far toward the top of the percentile in their understanding of the community and public relations needs for the team. Mecklenburg regularly was one of the last guys after a game to undress, instead sitting by his locker and patiently answering questions until the last reporter was done.

He was the Broncos' player representative during the strike of 1987, and there had been the usual amount of nasty mudslinging from both management and players. Meck worked hard to represent his side as well as possible against the colossal NFL PR machine, and finally the strike ended and the doors of the Broncos headquarters were opened to the players.

Not long after, Mecklenburg made his way across the practice field to where the Broncos' head of PR was standing. Meck extended his hand and said, "I'm sorry to have caused you so much trouble."

In reality, few players have ever caused a PR man as little trouble as he.

Mecklenburg had class, perspective, and balance as a player. "I don't know why some guys make it hard. They don't understand that when they retire from the game their resume is basically the goodwill they developed in the community, and no matter how much money you made, you still have to live there.

"The community thing is an opportunity, it's not a burden in any way. I can lend my name to a program or get involved with a program and all of a sudden it is making more money, or reaching more kids, or more sick people. It's a great opportunity, and guys should take more advantage of it than they do."

Chapter 18

SHANNON SHARPE

BEFORE THE BRONCOS

In the five decades of Denver Broncos history, there has never been a player to compare with Shannon Sharpe as a storyteller, as a nation of pro football fans is finding out by watching his weekly commentaries on CBS.

When one talks to Shannon Sharpe, one had better be prepared to do a lot of listening, too.

"I was born poor and grew up poor," Sharpe says. "Born in Chicago, grew up in Georgia, kind of a rural area, went to high school, played sports, and above all, all the time, tried to do everything my brother did." Shannon's older brother Sterling played for the Green Bay Packers before injuries cut his great career short and sent him into broadcasting.

"Everything Sterling did, I tried to do, and he was a great player. Eventually, I was a player in my own right, and the two of us are very close. We still talk all the time."

Shannon readily admits he was a natural when he started playing football and emulating his older brother.

"I didn't lift weights until I got to college and the thing was that I was just so much more gifted, more talented than everyone else. My brother really worked hard at football. I could have been really, really special in high school. You have to understand, football was my worst sport in high school. I only got one trophy in football growing up, and that was my senior year and I was the team's MVP. Other than that I was better at basketball, and the only reason I played football was because my brother played and I wanted to be like my brother. I wore the same number that he wore in high school, I wore the same number that he wore in college, and I wore the same number that he wore in the NFL. I wanted to be like him and that was the only reason that I played football.

"I was really focused on sports and was not what you would call a great student. Some people graduate magna cum laude, but when I graduated, it was more like, 'Thank you, Lordy!'"

After a spectacularly prolific pass-catching career at Savannah State, the Broncos made Sharpe their seventh-round draft choice in 1990, the 192nd player chosen that year and the last time in his career he would ever be selected for anything that late in a process.

Sharpe brought with him a drive and determination to succeed seldom seen before or since, in Denver or anywhere.

"It was just the way that I was raised. My grandfather and grandmother were big influences on my life, on how you do things, how to carry yourself, and I have always tried to carry myself in such a way that my family would be proud of me. I remember my grandfather telling me and my brother that he really didn't care what we became, as long as we never had to look him and my grandmother in the eye and say, 'I am sorry.' That was it. My grandmother is so proud now if she gets the opportunity to see us on television. She tells

---

Shannon Sharpe picks up extra yardage against the Chiefs in 1998. Four years later, Sharpe played the game of his life, catching 12 passes for 214 yards and two TDs against Kansas City. © *Eric Lars Bakke / Rich Clarkson and Associates*

me I talk too much and that she doesn't know why I talk so much and I tell her I get paid to talk. She says I don't let any of the other people talk. I know that she is proud of us, and that early discipline was a big factor in our development. When you are small, you don't understand why your parents or your grandparents are so hard on you, but that is the only chance they have. You just have one chance to rear a child; you don't get a second chance to do it."

THE SETTING

Shannon Sharpe hit the ground running when he got to Denver, and the motivating force of his whole career was the drive to greatness, and that was the setting for everything he did. Whatever he accomplished, he had his eye on improvement—on more and better—until there was no goal left.

Early on, he had to answer questions about his own role.

"'Do I really belong in the National Football League?' Sharpe remembers thinking. 'Do I really belong on the Denver Broncos to be so lucky and fortunate to catch passes from John Elway?' A lot of things could have happened differently. I am not so sure—and I tell people this all of the time—I am not so sure that I would have been drafted at all if Dan Reeves had not taken me in the seventh round. What if I'd gone to another team that was not so willing to work with me? I came in as a wide receiver but the tight ends got hurt and since I was the biggest wide receiver Dan said, 'What do you think about playing H-back/tight end?' I told him, 'If it is going to give me an opportunity to catch passes, if it is going to give me an opportunity to get on the field, then sure.'"

Once he got into the lineup, he never looked back.

"It is not that often that you see a guy that has all of the major records at one position (tight end)—yards, catches, touchdowns, and the most receiving yards in a game. Jerry Rice has the most receiving yards and the most touchdowns, and the most catches, but even he doesn't have the most yards in a game. The same thing for Emmitt Smith. I am one of the few guys. Dan Marino has the passing record,

SHANNON SHARPE AT A GLANCE

POSITION: Tight End
COLLEGE: Savannah State University
PLAYING HEIGHT, WEIGHT: 6-2, 228
YEARS PLAYED FOR BRONCOS: 1990-1999, 2002-2003
UNIFORM NUMBER: 84
NOTABLE: Shannon Sharpe is the NFL's all-time leader among tight
ends in receptions, reception yardage, and touchdowns. He holds
numerous Broncos and NFL reception records and was a vital ele-
ment of three world championship teams--two with the Broncos,
as well as one with the Baltimore Ravens. Sharpe went to the Pro
Bowl as a Bronco seven times, second only to John Elway among
offensive players in team history. Sharpe was inducted into the
Colorado Sports Hall of Fame in 2005 and upon future eligibility
is considered a very strong candidate for induction into the Pro
Football Hall of Fame.
THE GAME: Denver at Kansas City, October 20, 2002

but he doesn't have the most passing yards in a game. I have an awful
lot of the records."

And by the way, he could add, three world championships.

Every day, his leadership—both on and off the field—confidence,
cockiness, and obsessive drive rubbed off on the younger players.

Sharpe was weaving a career tapestry that without doubt will place
him in the Pro Football Hall of Fame.

"I played 14 years. A lot of times they use the excuse that someone
didn't play long enough, he didn't have longevity. And then there is,
well his numbers are okay, but they are not great. Then well, he didn't
win a Super Bowl. Really, I think in the grand scheme of things, when
you look back at my career, I had 14 years, and in 11 of those 14 years
I had 50-catch seasons—the only tight end to have ever done that. So
I really think if you look at my career and what I was able to do, I
make no apologies.

"I wish I could have played all 14 years with John Elway, then I
really would have loved to see my numbers. But the fact of the matter

is if you looked at when I played and you look at the numbers and compare them to the tight ends that I played with, I really think that it is an open-and-shut case. Ozzy Newsome and Kevin Winslow were great players, but from 1990 until when I walked out of that Broncos locker room in 2003, you would be hard pressed to show me a tight end that had better production than what I had.

"Ultimately, the Hall of Fame is out of my hands. But put it this way here…I auditioned for the part for 14 years. Whether or not I get the part, it is not up to me anymore. I auditioned and I had a great audition."

And he hit some pretty good notes in the audition.

"Really, the setting for the so-called game of my life was the setting of my life itself—what makes a man. For me, I got even deeper into the discipline, the lifting, dietary pattern.

"The way I looked at it was the thing that I never want to do was have regrets about my career. I was reading somewhere that you should never regret what you have done or what you said, because at one point in time that is exactly what you wanted to do. So when I said, 'I want to play this game for as long as I possibly can, and I never want to look back and say if I had eaten better, if I had worked out harder, if I had studied more, I might have, could have been an OK player.' I look back at my career and I don't think there was another catch, another yard, another touchdown, another Super Bowl that I could have won, because I did everything, as far as preparation, that was going to give me the best opportunity to be successful and help my football team win.

"I began to have those thoughts and develop them at about the end of the 1992 season. At that time I remember sitting down with John (Elway) late in the season. He had missed four games and had just come back. I remember he and I having a conversation and him telling me that I had an opportunity to be good. He said not just good, but really good. 'You have an opportunity to be special,' John said. And for John Elway to tell me that really impacted me. A coach saying it is one thing, but this was John Elway—a guy that had already taken the team to three Super Bowls and was thought of as one of the premier quarterbacks of the NFL. Here he is telling a seventh-round draft pick, 'You have special skills, you have a talent and you could be really, really unique in this league.'

"It was at that time that I made up my mind to work extremely hard in the off-season. I decided to completely redo my diet and leave no stone unturned in my preparation, and that was going to give me the best opportunity to be successful. From that moment on I really truly put my whole, entire, absolute focus on football."

He carried this structure and discipline into every aspect of his life. "Structure, discipline and organization can be great qualities if properly utilized. Would I call myself an obsessive-compulsive guy? Yes, in a good sense. If you are able to control it and it doesn't take you to a psychologist. I have been able to use it as strength.

"Hey, it was never just me, though. It never can be. We play with people, we are coached by people."

And in that regard, Sharpe is quick to credit Mike Shanahan for helping to develop his abilities from raw talent into unquestioned greatness.

"Mike encouraged me to take my game to another level."

Sharpe was never thought of as a blocker, but when the Broncos won back-to-back world championships he was cited as a key blocker in Denver's vaunted running game, particularly in the Super Bowl XXXII win over Green Bay.

"When Mike came in he basically told me, 'Shannon we are going to need you to catch less and block more.' At the time I was just starting to get my niche in the National Football League and I put together back-to-back really good 80-catch seasons. I got my first 1,000-yard receiving season, which is big for a tight end. There are not many tight ends who can say they caught for 1,000 yards in a particular season. So I was really starting to develop my own identity in the NFL, and now you have a new coach coming in and saying, 'OK, now we are going to pull the reins back a little bit and we want you to catch less in order for us to be the type of team that we need to be.' And he said, 'You know, I think that instead of catching in the high 80s, maybe you can catch in the mid-60s or low 70s.' I realized that was going to give me an opportunity to win a Super Bowl because at that point in time I had gone to three Pro Bowls, had a 1,000-yard season, so now the only way to really top it off was to get to and win a Super Bowl. So after sitting down and thinking about it, it really was a no-brainer, because when it is all said and done, that is how you want to be remembered. You want to be a guy that has won a championship, and I think to win multiple championships really makes a huge statement about a career."

Sharpe had a degree of preparedness that permeated every aspect of his life. Like all teams, the Broncos have catered lunches for the players during the work week, but Sharpe would routinely skip the catered food on Wednesday and Thursday and instead eat what he brought from home—generally something akin to chicken (no skin) and green beans, no dessert.

He took his lifting regimen to such a level that he ultimately was featured on the cover of muscle magazines, and his firm focus was mental as well as physical.

"I am a big reader and I keep a lot of quotes. When Mike would give us the first 15 or the first 12 plays for the game I would always write a quote on my paper and it was always what I was thinking at that particular time. I am very analytical and I think about things and always compare things and a lot of the time people probably don't think about things the way that I think about them. But once they hear me and they see what I am comparing it to they think about it and say that it does make a lot of sense.

"I would always write a 'January return' theme on a daily basis, which means if you want to be playing in January you have to pay the price in September, October, November, and December on a daily basis. On every Tuesday, I was always over there on the players' day off. I had to be there, to satisfy myself, not to satisfy coaches. A lot of the coaches never saw me, but I would say, 'You know what? I didn't get better today and I could have.'"

And not only did Denver win, but it won big right away. The Broncos won Super Bowl XXXII over the Packers following the 1997 season and went undefeated for a calendar year before losing two games late in 1998. They then surged through the playoffs and won Super Bowl XXXIII over the Atlanta Falcons.

THE GAME OF MY LIFE

"I remember catching a touchdown pass in my first game ever at Kansas City, and it was at that moment I knew that I belonged in the National Football League."

And then, on October 20, 2002, in his 13th season of pro football, Shape indelibly put a permanent mark in the NFL's single-game record book.

He caught 12 passes for 214 yards, the most receiving yards by a tight end in NFL history, breaking a record that had stood for 39 years. (Jackie Smith had 212 for the Rams vs. Pittsburgh on October 13, 1963.) Always one for the exclamation point, Sharpe also scored twice that day, including one touchdown that covered 82 yards from scrimmage.

"As I look at my entire football career, there have been so many high spots, so many great moments and games, it is difficult to pinpoint one special day. But we are weaving the tapestry of my football life here, and that game was the icing on the cake in terms of the records that I was fortunate enough to set. Plus, and most of all, the Chiefs were a big rival, and we won that game, 37-34 in Kansas City.

"It is very tough to win in Kansas City, and we trailed three different times in that game, so to come back and win it on their home turf was particularly gratifying. One of my touchdowns, the 82-yard play, tied the game at 13-13, and the other helped us come back for good and win it in the fourth quarter.

"People would always say, 'Why do you work so hard during the season or the off-season?' Because I think someone out there is trying to get better than me. There is some tight end out there that wants my job; there is some tight end in the NFL who thinks he can be better than Shannon Sharpe, and I didn't want that to happen. No matter how long I would play, whether it would be five years or 15 years, I wanted people to respect what I did and say, 'You know what? This guy can still play. Yeah, he is 33; yeah, he is 35. But that guy can still play and we have to account for it.'

"I was 34 when I set that record in Kansas City. A whole lot of guys come and go and are retired by the time they are 34. Pro football is a young man's game. But I took great pride in being the best, in winning. I was very, very competitive, and I set that record at the age of 34. And that's why I worked out so hard in the off-season. You never know when a moment will come, but it comes quickly, and it is up to you to be ready for it.

"That was one of the few times that I can say we beat Kansas City in Kansas City. You know Kansas City, no matter what their record is, they are very tough at home. Very, very tough, and it is also the team that I scored my very first touchdown against. I was aware of that at the time, absolutely."

"At the time it was happening, I had no idea I had that many yards. I remember in the first half, I had only caught three passes and I had been such a big part of the game plan earlier in the week at practice and then to come out in the first half and have only three catches for 34 yards. I was thinking, 'Oh well,' and we were losing. So I was thinking it was going to be one of those days where I'd have six catches for 65-70 yards and we'd lose the ball game.

"Then we went into the locker room and Gary (Kubiak, offensive coordinator) was at the board and he said, 'Look we have got to have guys that are going to step up and make plays. There is no secret here and we don't have any magic plays that we are going to come out with to get a touchdown. We have got to throw the ball better, we have got to catch the ball better, we have got to block better, we have got to run better.' And low and behold, he said we were going to come out with this play, and I liked the play. It was a counter pass and I thought, 'You know what? I just hope that when we call this play they will be in the right coverage.'

"Sure enough, they were in a cover-two and we ran a counter-pass. The linebacker took one step and basically that was all that I needed, because at the snap of the ball I was gone. If he takes one step, the thing is: If you are even, you're leavin'. And I got even. Brian Griese made a perfect throw and it was off to the races. That was really the start of it.

"I think that Mike had a lot to do with it. One thing that you know when you play with Mike Shanahan: If you are a receiver or if you are a running back, he is going to go to the hot hand. So at any point in time of the game, no matter what the game calls for, if he is throwing you the football and you have made some tough plays and got the ball in the end zone, then he is going to continue to feed you.

"They led in the first quarter, led by 10 in the second quarter, led at the half, and led until we finally tied it with 21 seconds left in the game. We won it in overtime.

"Like I said, if things are going well, Mike will go with the hot hand, and in the second half I had nine catches for 180 yards and two touchdowns. It is always great to win, always great to win on the road, always great to beat one of your top rivals. Having a major role in the win and breaking a 39-year-old pro football record in the process makes for a very memorable day."

AFTER THE CHEERING STOPPED

Sharpe played 14 great years in the NFL, and he became as known for his quick wit and engaging conversation among media members as for his Hall of Fame play, so it was natural that television would soon come calling, and CBS did so immediately. Sharpe quickly made his mark as a studio analyst for CBS, and his loquacious style became a national hit.

"In my 14 years, football was it. Nothing else mattered to me. It is something that I have to be honest about—I wasn't the greatest brother, I wasn't the greatest son, and I wasn't the greatest father. I am not going to sit here and make any apologies for that, because football was my life. It consumed me and there was not one day that I didn't think about football. There was not one day in my 14 years that I did not think about how I could get better or what can I do to help the football team to become better. I knew it was time for me to go because when CBS called me, it was the first time in 14 years that I thought about something other than football. At no time during those 14 years did I ever think about something other than football.

"There had been some contacts of that type earlier, with some people calling, and I talked to my agent Marvin Demoff and told him, 'No, I am not ready yet.' So earlier, I did not even entertain the thought, but at that moment something other than football interested me, so I thought about something else."

He has taken the same attitude he had as a player into his new career.

Although still close to the NFL, he acknowledges, "It is a bit different now because I just left the game three years ago and a lot of these guys that I am talking about are people who I played with and against. Sometimes I am talking favorably about them and sometimes I am criticizing, so it gets hard at times. But I say to the guys, 'Look, never take what I say personal. This is what my opinion is from when I look at you from the game or from when I watch tape and I see better than I hear. I know what the coaches are saying, I know what the players are saying but that is not what I am seeing, so something is not adding up.'

"Sometimes players, fans and critics get after an analyst, saying that he didn't even play the game, so how does he know what he is talking about? Or he played but he wasn't that good, or what did he ever win? But they can't say that to me because I played 14 years, I won Super Bowls, I went to Pro Bowls. I was thought of at one point in time during my career as being the best tight end in football, so they know that at the end of the day I know what I am talking about. Coaches know I know what I am talking about, and I am expected to be totally honest, which is how I have always been. So it is a natural thing for me. I am sure there are guys that don't like what I am saying—no one really likes to be criticized—but at the end of the day you do your job, allow me to do mine, and we will be fine."

He admits there is an entirely different type of preparation in the TV world. Sharpe notes, "You have to read a lot. You have to see what the beat writers are writing in the paper. Get on the Internet and see what somebody else is saying, and then I try and watch film and see for myself. I want to see what is going on. I know what I am looking for. I had to watch film and study as a player, so this is just another version of the same task.

"I always want to get better, I don't care what I'm doing. I keep a book of philosophy beside my bed, and I look at it almost every night before I go to bed, if you can believe that. It's by the German philosopher, Friedrich Nietzsche.

"The best quote I have seen—and I have kept this quote for 20 years and have written it down on several different things—is by Samuel Johnson. 'Almost every man wastes part of his life in attempts to display qualities which he does not possess, and to gain applause which he cannot keep.'"

When attitude, hard work, and preparation meet opportunity, something very special can happen. Shannon Sharpe has maximized that theory in his life and career.

And as always, he has the final word. "I never want to be the kind of guy who complains about the noise when opportunity knocks."

Chapter 19

TERRELL DAVIS

BEFORE THE BRONCOS

Terrell Davis grew up as one of six brothers in his San Diego family. "My mother, father, and every brother had a part in me being who I was. It had some eventual influence on me being a player, but initially it made me the young man that I was."

With five brothers, he had to grow up tough. "They were all older than I was. I had to fight and fend for myself and never had anything easy. I think that in itself taught me how to be tough. And then the way my dad raised me, he was a disciplinarian type of father, so I didn't get into a lot of trouble growing up. And my mother's a very caring, loving woman. She gave me the nurturing side, so all that played a role in me growing up," Davis explains. "You take the values that you learn early in life onto the field. I just applied them to situations on the field. I always thought there was nothing on the football field that I ran into that came close to being tougher than what I experienced in life."

At Lincoln High School in San Diego he played nose guard, fullback, linebacker, and was the kicker. What about running back?

"When I came to Lincoln High School, they already had two running backs there that were already established. That was number one. Number two was, I didn't really want to be a running back," the future superstar remembers. "Although prior to me playing high school football, I was legendary in little league football as a running back."

Davis served primarily as a defensive lineman. "I thought that was great. I didn't have to be the guy who had to have the spotlight on him every game."

But he points out a psychological factor at work as well. "Really, in high school, the one thing I thought—and I didn't think it was possible—was that some people are scared to succeed. And in high school, I was one of those guys who—I knew I could be a good running back—I just didn't want to play. I was scared. If I performed as a running back, I would have to do that job or perform like that week in and week out, and I wasn't ready for that."

But eventually he found his way to running back and was soon recruited by George Allen to go to Long Beach State.

He pointed out that he had an array of skills as a back. "My blocking skills were phenomenal. I had pretty good hands, and when I ran with the football, I caught the eye of George Allen. When he came in, he was the only school that recruited me.

"At Long Beach State, after I left high school, I said, 'You know what? I've got to stop holding back this fear of succeeding.' I only played probably six games at Long Beach State, and I led the team in rushing."

Davis was doing well at Long Beach State until bad news rocked his world. "One day I was walking across campus and somebody

---

A sixth-round draft pick in 1995, Terrell Davis was invaluable on consecutive world championship Broncos teams in 1997 and 1998 and became only the fourth player in NFL history to rush for 2,000 yards.
© David Gonzales/Rich Clarkson and Associates

stopped me and said, 'Hey, did you hear that the school is dropping football?'"

Just like that, Davis had no team.

However, Georgia had watched tape of the developing youngster and offered him a scholarship.

"I knew I had talent. It was just a matter of my confidence and having the willingness to carry that load and be that guy who performs like that. Georgia came and got me. I played in Georgia, and the rest is history.

"My last two games of my career were probably the best games I had at Georgia. One was against Georgia Tech, and one was against Auburn, which was undefeated. I had 140 or 150 yards in both of those games. I think those two games alone got me invited to the Blue-Gray game. That's how Mike Shanahan and (Broncos offensive coordinator) Gary Kubiak got a chance to see me."

He had run well for the Bulldogs, but an injury and the Georgia staff's desire to pass the ball more dropped his draft status, and Shanahan scooped Davis up with the team's sixth-round selection.

THE SETTING

"When I came here, I knew I was a player. It was just a case of doing what I could do in the situation, absolutely. If you talk to anybody who's drafted in the lower rounds, you'd be hard pressed to find anybody who thinks of themselves as a late-round talent. Everyone thinks they're a number-one draft pick."

When Davis got to Denver, he saw the kind of offense they ran and realized he had a chance to fit in fast. "It was pretty much what I did at Georgia. I blocked a lot, caught a lot of passes, and played in a pretty pass-happy offense in college. It really polished my skills up. I could already block because I was a fullback in high school, so blocking was nothing new to me, but catching passes was at Georgia. So when I came to Denver, it was a natural fit—the passing, the pass-catching, the blocking, the running. And I was further along the curve than they probably expected me to be."

TERRELL DAVIS AT A GLANCE

POSITION: Running Back
COLLEGE: University of Georgia
PLAYING HEIGHT, WEIGHT: 5-11, 210
YEARS PLAYED FOR BRONCOS: 1995-2002
UNIFORM NUMBER: 30
NOTABLE: Terrell Davis was named the NFL Most Valuable Player in 1998, was Offensive Player of the Year and started his third straight Pro Bowl game after a campaign in which he led the NFL in both rushing and touchdowns. He was named Player of the Year by numerous organizations after a campaign in which he became the fourth 2,000-yard rusher in NFL history. In the postseason he extended his NFL-record streak of 100-yard rushing performances to seven straight games, all Denver victories, a feat unmatched previously and a record which will be extremely difficult to surpass. He helped lead Denver to a second consecutive world championship in 1998 after being named Super Bowl XXXII Most Valuable Player the previous year. Davis is considered a candidate for the Pro Football Hall of Fame and was inducted into the Colorado Sports Hall of Fame in 2004.
THE GAME: Super Bowl XXXII, Denver vs. Green Bay, January 25, 1998, San Diego, California

He became a starter by the opening game of his rookie year and rushed for 1,117 yards in that 1995 campaign, turning it up to 1,538 yards, with 13 rushing touchdowns, in his second pro campaign.

"It was just a perfect fit," Davis acknowledges. "Coming to a situation with a new head coach bringing a lot of very solid philosophies to the game, playing with John Elway and Shannon Sharpe, and then having the guys around us, it was really a perfect fit."

And he fit in well, running the ball and becoming a focal point of the Broncos' offense, which now featured a running back to complement the legendary Elway.

Denver went 13-3 in 1996, setting the table for what was to come. But first there was a huge upset loss at home to Jacksonville to erase the Broncos' hopes for 1996.

"What that game did for me and, I believe, the rest of the team was it made us realize that just because on paper we look like a pretty good team, we have to come to play," Davis explains. "It almost took our chance of winning a championship away because that's what I thought when we lost that game. We blew it. We blew our opportunity. We knew it would be tough to get back in that situation, but then when we came into camp the next year, there was something about the way we approached the training camp. There was sort of a swagger, sort of, 'OK, we know where we got to last year. We know what to expect now, and we're not going to take anybody lightly this time. Now it's time to come play.'"

The Broncos had a great regular season in 1997, but it was a strong year in the AFC West, and so their 12-4 record put them into the NFL playoffs as a wild card. A home win over Jacksonville and road victories at Kansas City and Pittsburgh took the Denver franchise to its fifth Super Bowl game.

The Broncos had never won one, and they were huge underdogs to the world champion Green Bay Packers. The site for the game was Terrell Davis' hometown of San Diego. "I was going home to play in the Super Bowl. It was every kid's dream come true."

That, and a lot more, rang true as events unfolded.

THE GAME OF MY LIFE

According to Davis, that week in his hometown was fun. "It was busy; it was exciting, it was draining, at the same time. I was trying not to lose focus. You've got people patting you on the back before you even play the game, and they're excited about you coming home. But still, there's a game that has to be played. I was ear to ear that whole week. I was smiling. I'm at the house—all my family, all my friends, all week."

He even had his Lincoln High School jersey retired at a mid-week school assembly. "Oh man, it was fun," Davis understates. Very few guys have returned to their high schools as bigger heroes than Terrell Davis did that day. "That was cool. I didn't do much in high school as a player, and then they retired my jersey. That was very flattering, and I could not help but think how far I had come."

Shanahan had done extensive film study of the Packers and knew that the development of his gifted young running back gave the Broncos a far better chance to win than previous Denver clubs had enjoyed. The Broncos knew they could run the ball effectively against anyone.

The NFC team had won 13 straight Super Bowl games, but this one would feature an AFC team using the powerful running game that had become a trademark of the senior conference.

"We were big underdogs against the Packers, but somehow, the way our team was playing, we didn't feel like an underdog. That's exactly how we felt. Again, playing on the team we had, our mentality was that we will put 30 points on the board on anybody. We wanted to just beat people up, dominate them, and that's what we felt we could do. I understood why we were underdogs, but that didn't affect the way we felt. Number one, we were an AFC team. An AFC team hadn't beaten an NFC team in 13 years. We were the Broncos, who had been there a few other times and never got the job done. So I understood why we were underdogs, but we knew we were not underdogs. We just had to go out there and show people. We could show you better than we could tell you, and we knew it."

The Packers scored first, but then Denver took the ball right down the field on its first drive, with Davis scoring the first of his three touchdowns. But late in the first quarter, Davis suffered an injury.

The star running back had been kicked in the head and had the signs of a migraine headache, a condition for which Davis took medicine regularly. The team trainer said he would be back in the game, so it was announced that he was "probable" to return to the game. The team felt that the migraine condition could be controlled.

The televising network and entire press corps needed to be brought up to date on Davis' condition; however, there was no reason to alarm anyone by using the word "migraine" unless further medical testing determined that he in fact had a migraine headache. The trainers were certain of his return, so his status was reported as probable.

Davis explains, "I got kneed in the head late in the first quarter. Typically, when I get a migraine, it starts off by having these visual problems. They're called auras. When I got kicked in the head, I left the game for a play or two. It takes a few minutes before the actual condition where I can't see kicks in. So then that happened in the early second quarter. Then that's when I told Mike (Shanahan), and I told Greek (trainer Steve Antonopulos) that I was experiencing symptoms of a migraine headache, I couldn't see.

"But by then we had driven down to the Green Bay goal line, and Mike wanted Elway to run after faking to me. And of course, I have to be in, or the fake won't work. That's when Mike tells me, 'Just go in on this play. If you don't stay in, they won't believe we're going to run it.' So I went in there."

Thus Davis went back in for just that one second-quarter play, a one-yard touchdown run by Elway that worked because of the initial fake to the brilliant running back. Denver was ahead 14-7, and would add a field goal with Davis still out of the lineup.

"My whole thing, my whole mind-set that entire time was, 'Man, this is the wrong time to get a migraine.' I was begging God, 'Please, this is the wrong time for this.'

"I stood on the sideline for a minute, and Mike told me to go into the locker room. I went into the locker room and took my medication. The medicine really makes the headache portion a lot less intense. It really makes it to where it's a subtle headache, but it's not full-blown like a migraine. But I can work with a subtle headache versus a full-blown headache. It was like a mild headache. If I had a full migraine, there was probably no way I could've finished that game."

Even with a headache that nearly sidelined him for the second half, Terrell Davis zips untouched into the end zone for the winning touchdown against the Packers in Super Bowl XXXII, the game of his life.
© Rich Clarkson/Rich Clarkson and Associates

Davis was back in the lineup for the Broncos' first possession of the second half. On his first carry, he fumbled. And that would be the last bad thing to happen to Terrell Davis in Super Bowl XXXII.

This game ultimately belonged to Davis and the superb Denver offensive line. Green Bay's massive defensive tackle Gilbert Brown was dominated by center Tom Nalen and guards Mark Schlereth and Brian Habib, allowing Davis to run up the middle throughout the remainder of the night.

As the Broncos had more and more success up the middle, it also opened up the outside running game for Davis, who would finish with three running touchdowns and the Super Bowl XXXII Most Valuable Player award.

"I think we surprised everybody because they had Gilbert Brown and some other big men up front defensively. Our game plan was what we did most of the year. We relied on the running game heavily, and we threw the ball on top of our run. That's what we did. We came out there and did what we were doing best. We ran the football. And I knew that. I knew going into that game that our only chance to beat this team is to stick with our guns. Our guns were running the football and pounding people, wearing them down, and eating up clock, controlling the clock, keeping their offense off the field, and letting our defense rest."

The Broncos scored 31 points on the four rushing touchdowns and a Jason Elam field goal. Davis adds, "It was not only the clock, but putting points on the board when we had an opportunity. When we got the ball, we did all that. We controlled the clock. We controlled the ground. We took our shots with the passing game at times, but our main bread and butter was to run the football. And then we did some things with slot formations to keep (the Packers') La'Roi Glover from sticking his nose so far down into the box.

"The game plan was a beautiful game plan that whole week. And you can feel it when Mike puts in the game plan some weeks and you talk to some of the players, and the defensive guys might be like, 'Man, we're going to shut them down.' Same thing for our offense. You get a sense just by the type of packages we put in, what type of plays we run during the week, you get a sense of how successful the game is going to be."

Davis says the entire offense could feel this one coming. "Number one, it was the Super Bowl, so there was no other option. This was for all the marbles. But then on top of that, the game plan was solid all week. We weren't trying to do tricky stuff. I don't like any plays where you get outside of what you do and try to trick people. I don't believe in that. I believe in sticking with what we do, and that's what we did. We didn't try any trick plays. We did what the Broncos do best, and we ran the football."

The Broncos ran for 179 yards, despite gaining none on the ground in the second period, which Davis sat out with blurred vision.

He acknowledges the surreal aspects of Denver's win. "If it had been a movie, critics would say it's unbelievable. I mean, a guy is going to go play in the Super Bowl in his hometown, where he went to high school, and he's going to be the Super Bowl MVP, after coming back from the onset of a migraine headache.

"Everything that you could wish for, if you tried to put together a perfect scenario, I don't know if I could've done that situation any better. It even came with some drama with the migraine headache. It really was a storybook type of win. The entire season culminated around that one week."

After the defense held off the final Green Bay drive and the offense took the field to run out the clock, Davis reflected on what had just transpired. "I thought, 'You've got three touchdowns. You're in your hometown. You're playing before family, friends, international TV.' The gratification and satisfaction of winning that first Super Bowl, and being MVP in my hometown—it was an awful lot to absorb.

"I don't know if anybody's ever done this before, but what I tried to do before the game was I tried to make the game—after all the hype, after visiting my high school, after realizing this is the Super Bowl—like any other game and not get caught up into all the off-field activities and festivities. In my mind, it had already switched gears into being a regular-type game—a regular game, but not just a regular game. I tried to reduce any distractions.

"It doesn't hit you until days later what has just happened because you're sitting there like, 'We just won the Super Bowl.' Physically, you don't feel any different. But you're trying to get your mind to catch up with what just happened because it's a game and the game is over. You see the confetti. You go to the little podium. You speak. You've got the trophy, and you're holding it. You're with your teammates. You're having a great time. And then all of a sudden, it's over. It's over. Everybody's gone. Everybody's left the locker room.

"You're back at the hotel, and you really just want to sit around there and let it soak in because it hasn't hit you yet. That's what happens right after the game. For me, I was still a little sick and still a little woozy, so I didn't even go out. I was exhausted, so I went back to the hotel room, and I saw my family downstairs and spoke to them briefly after the game. We shared and celebrated a little bit, but then after that I went up to the room and ordered room service and, basically, I went to bed."

So while the Denver Broncos family was having the greatest party in franchise history, the Super Bowl MVP running back was having room service.

"Yeah, that's right. I came down to the party, got my family into the party. I stayed with them for probably 15, 20 minutes, and then I went upstairs. I was just exhausted. I was still feeling that headache a bit, so I went upstairs and ordered room service. I turned on the news, and I was watching the highlights of the game over and over and over until I fell asleep."

History has shown that Davis was a pivotal performer on one of the greatest teams of modern pro football history, one that would set an NFL record with 34 wins in three years (1996-98) and that ultimately would go an entire calendar year without a loss (December 1997-December 1998).

Davis puts his stamp of concurrence on that evaluation. "I'm not saying we were the only great team, but I believe history will show us to be one of 10 or 15 great teams that have existed in the National Football League. I look back on that quite often. The more that people talk about it and they ask me questions about the '98 team and I look back on it, we did some great things."

AFTER THE CHEERING STOPPED

A knee injury cut his brilliant career short while he was still in his prime, but Davis adjusted without regrets and now lives in San Diego, where he works in real estate and does some work as an analyst for the NFL Network as well.

"I don't have any ill feelings about my career ending short. I played seven years. I was pretty beat up the last three, but I was in the league for seven years. There are some guys who don't see a year, two years in this league. Now, I wish I could've played 10 years, maybe more, but at the same time, I look at what I was able to accomplish and I say, 'Wow, there's nothing that I did not achieve,' and so that keeps me at peace. When I think about how much I did play, I say, 'Well, I won two championships, and I've got a rushing title. I've got a 2,000-yard season, Super Bowl MVP and league MVP. Very few guys have ever done that."

His work with the NFL Network takes him away from his home several times a year, as he stays close to the game doing interviews with players and offering commentary on the game from the network's Los Angeles studio.

Davis enjoys playing golf for recreation, stays close to his family and friends from football, and he never looks back with regret.

"I choose to live with what happened, not with what might have happened. You can only have a great life. It's like a sunset. When it's beautiful, it's beautiful. We should take the time to enjoy it."

Chapter 20

JOHN ELWAY

BEFORE THE BRONCOS

John Elway is a coach's son, and to know the coach was to know the son. Jack Elway built the engine that would power the juggernaut that his quarterback son would become.

Along with the morning Wheaties, the Elway kids got a daily dose of team values as a coach sees them. Passion for the game, leadership, integrity, fair play, and a competitive spirit were absorbed at the highest possible level by a young son who acknowledges, "My dad was, and is, my hero."

"I was fortunate to have great parents. My mom was always there for me and my two sisters, running the household while my dad was busy coaching. And as he moved up the college coaching ladder, the family naturally had a few moves."

When Jack took a job in the Los Angeles area he knew where his priorities lay, with a strong-armed and strong-willed son of whom he once said to wife Jan: "Sometimes I wonder if this kid is actually as good as I think he is."

Jack found the high school for John before finding the house for his family, and there was only one great choice.

Young John was a high school sophomore. "Football was not at the top of my list because I had experienced a run-oriented offense and had not yet experienced the fun of throwing the football," he says.

But Jack settled on Granada Hills High School and took him to meet the coach.

At Granada Hills, the legendary Jack Neumeier had been running the West Coast offense since the mid-1970s, several years before it was "discovered" by the pros. Neumeier talked to young Elway about the passing game. "That's where my love of the game began," he remembers. "Coach Neumeier said, 'My deal is this: If I ever call two straight running plays, you come to the sideline, hand me your helmet, and I'll understand. If we are at the two-yard line, and I call two straight running plays, the same deal applies.'"

Deal accepted, and arguably the greatest quarterback in football history was on his way.

"Coach Neumeier was a great coach, a genius of offensive football, and he was a fine man. I was honored to have played for him," Elway notes.

"Even though my dad was coaching at San Jose State, he thought Stanford would be a better school for me." So Elway went to The Farm in Palo Alto, where the legend of his skills preceded him his freshman year.

After a Stanford-San Jose State game in which Jack's Spartans got the best of the Cardinal, the senior Elway told his son, "You're riding home with me." Queried by John as to why that was necessary, Jack said, "Because if you don't come with me, your mom will never let me in the door."

Elway threw 77 touchdown passes at Stanford while setting an NCAA record for the lowest percentage of passes intercepted in a

Finally banishing all thoughts of him as the quarterback who could never "win the big one," John Elway led the Broncos to victory over the Packers in the game of his life—Super Bowl XXXII. © David Gonzales/Rich Clarkson and Associates

career. A consensus All-American as a senior, he set virtually every Pac-10 and Stanford career record for total offense and passing.

Very few people know that John Elway actually was not on scholarship for his final two seasons at Stanford.

A great baseball player as well, he signed with the New York Yankees and played one summer for their Oneonta (N.Y.) single-A farm club in 1982, hitting .318 while leading the club in runs batted in. "But NCAA rules at the time were such that if a player signed a pro contract in any sport, he lost his college scholarship," he explains.

So signing with the Yankees as their number-one draft choice in 1981 actually forced one of the greatest players in college football history to pay his own tuition for his final two years.

"It was a great experience, though, and I have no regrets. We have to be open to a lot of different things in life. I had a different number for home and road games, but one of my uniform numbers was number eight, which of course Yogi Berra wore, so I thought that was really cool!"

Elway went into the 1983 NFL draft not only as the highest-rated player in the country, but as the highest-rated quarterback since Joe Namath two decades earlier.

THE SETTING

He came to the Broncos amidst the greatest hype in modern pro football, and in no time transcended the hype and jumped into greatness.

The Broncos went 13-3 in his second season, and Elway carried the Broncos on his broad shoulders to three Super Bowls in four years—Super Bowl XXI in 1986, Super Bowl XXII in 1987, and Super Bowl XXIV in 1989. He had been in pro football for seven years, and had started in three Super Bowl games. Ultimately, he would be the only quarterback in history to start five.

But the problem with the first three was that Denver simply did not have enough talent to go around, and the Broncos lost all three

JOHN ELWAY AT A GLANCE

POSITION: Quarterback
COLLEGE: Stanford University
PLAYING HEIGHT, WEIGHT: 6-3, 215
YEARS PLAYED FOR BRONCOS: 1983-98
UNIFORM NUMBER: 7 (retired)
NOTABLE: Inducted into the Pro Football Hall of Fame on August
8, 2004, John Elway is universally regarded as one of the greatest
quarterbacks ever to play the game. The Denver Broncos retired
his jersey on September 13, 1999, and he was inducted into the
team's Ring of Fame on the same date. He was named the Most
Valuable Player of Super Bowl XXXIII, leading the Broncos to their
second consecutive world championship in that game. He retired
as the NFL's all-time winningest quarterback (148 wins), and was
voted to a franchise-record nine Pro Bowls, tied with Dan Marino
for the most ever by a quarterback. Elway was the NFL Most
Valuable Player in 1987 and the AFC Player of the Year in 1993.
The Edge NFL Man of the Year in 1992, he was named to the
Colorado Sports Hall of Fame in 1999, and was first-team on the
NFL's All-Decade team for the 1990s. Elway is pro football's all-
time leader in fourth-quarter game-saving/game-winning drives
with 47. He started 2,595 drives as a pro and was replaced just
10 times due to injury (.039%).
THE GAME: Super Bowl XXXII, Green Bay vs. Denver, January 25,
1998, San Diego, California

games, creating a completely unfair but nevertheless pervasive thought that he could not "win the big one."

It was pointed out that he really deserved to win a title and all that goes with it, but Elway said, "Deserve has got nothing to do with it. I am going to keep after it, and maybe next time we'll win it."

He continues, "There is not always a direct correlation in what you get out of what you put into something. However, you never relinquish your obligation to your talents, the hard work that you did, and the teaching and sacrifices that others have made on your behalf."

Elway always knew he carried the weight and expectations of the city on his shoulders, and after a pounding by San Francisco in the third of those title games, he commented to teammates, "They will never, ever forgive me for this."

Still, he persevered, just as his dad always advised him to do. By this time Jack had retired from active coaching and was himself a member of the Broncos organization in the team's personnel department.

In that role, Jack was a confidante not just to his son, but seemingly to everyone in the organization, imparting wisdom, wit, and philosophy to live by while watching practice or film.

"I would ask my dad, 'Can I still do this? Am I still good enough?'" Elway recalls. And Elway the older would continue to reply in the affirmative. "I made him promise that he would tell me if the day came when my skills had slipped, and I knew I could trust him above all others."

The Broncos went back to the AFC title game in 1991, losing at Buffalo, and then the franchise ebbed for a few years despite Elway's perpetual assault on the NFL and Broncos record books.

He kept his disappointment inside and just kept working. "Doing your best, making your absolute best effort to win at all times, in all situations, and never, ever giving up, is all you can do, and what you must continue to do. But the results sometimes come in varying degrees. You never know what is coming or how, so you have to keep working to the max all the time so you are ready for it when it comes."

Elway had enjoyed great success earlier with Mike Shanahan on the Broncos' staff as a mentor and offensive coordinator, and Shanahan returned to Denver in 1995, fresh from another championship win by San Francisco.

Shanahan aggressively added free-agent players and hit on some big-time draft choices, including running back Terrell Davis.

The Broncos went 8-8 in 1995, but followed that up with a 13-3 mark the following year before being upset in the playoffs at home by Jacksonville. However, the team was returning intact, sending out strong signals that they were ready to make another run.

The 1997 season came, and during a preseason game in Mexico City, Elway had to leave the game when the tendon in his right biceps popped loose.

"At first, it really scared me. I really didn't know what to expect because no other quarterback had ever experienced or thrown with a torn biceps tendon."

The entire city held its breath.

Nevertheless, eight days later he was able to throw with zip and accuracy, and the 15-year NFL signal caller pronounced himself ready to play.

The Broncos had a great regular season, but a tough loss at Kansas City doomed them to wild-card status as the playoffs began.

"We knew how good we were. We knew we were good enough to win the Super Bowl. That's all we cared about. We really did not focus on whether we were at home or not, just on playing like we knew we could."

They began the playoffs with a trouncing of the Jacksonville Jaguars at home, then the revenge tour continued as they went on the road and won a great game at Kansas City, setting up a visit to Pittsburgh for the AFC Championship Game. The Broncos beat the Steelers to advance to Elway's fourth Super Bowl game.

Only one wild-card team had ever won the Super Bowl—the 1980 Oakland Raiders—and the AFC was taking a 13-game losing streak into the game at San Diego. Added to the mix was the fact that Denver was to play the defending world champion Green Bay Packers, who had been installed as the heaviest favorite since Super Bowl III when Baltimore had a huge advantage over the New York Jets.

John Elway was about to take a leap from mere greatness to legend.

THE GAME OF MY LIFE

Make no mistake about it, the entire nation viewed this as John Elway's Super Bowl.

"We were a big underdog, but we had a tremendous amount of confidence. We were very sure that we had a tremendous team, and we just exuded confidence all week, but we had to tone down our comments all week long. There was no doubt in our mind that we would play great.

"Naturally, lots of family and friends came to the game. My sister and her family came down to San Diego on Friday. My nephew Patrick said, 'Uncle John, we don't care if you lose.' I said, 'You promise you'll let me back in your house?' And he said he would still let me in. I just put that in the back of my mind and said, 'Let's just go out and play the best game we can.'"

The Broncos went into this game as the most offensively balanced Denver team to play in the big game. Denver's offensive line and running game took over the contest.

The Packers scored first, but Denver answered with a long drive that culminated in a one-yard touchdown run by the game's eventual MVP, running back Terrell Davis.

Elway says he had no doubt about what the Broncos could do on the ground. "In my book, Terrell Davis was the best running back in the league, bar none. He showed it again in the most important game in franchise history. He was always breaking tackles, and he was always going north and south. He was really a load for the Packers."

Denver turned two Packers turnovers into 10 more points in the second quarter, giving Denver a 17-7 lead.

"They changed up a little bit on the D-line. A couple of their players went down and they were bringing different people in. They were always a big substitution team anyway. It really didn't concern us. We knew we were going to have to block a bunch of different looks. And we knew we could. We really had great confidence in our running game against the Packers that day."

Green Bay pulled into a 17-17 third-period tie, setting the stage for one of the most emotional moments in Super Bowl history.

Elway's passing stats for the game were nothing special (12-of-22 for 123 yards), but his poise and leadership were absolutes. Nothing epitomized that leadership more than the play that set up Denver's third touchdown. He remembers, "We had driven down to the Green Bay 12. It had been a long drive, but we were looking at a third-and-six. There was no way I wanted to settle for a field goal in this situation; I felt we had to get back up by seven. I dropped back to pass, but their secondary was doing a good job. As I dropped back, I saw just a crack on our right side, just enough space that I thought I could run, so I took off. They closed fast, so as I got near the first-down marker I leaped into the air, got hit pretty good and completely spun around in mid-air."

It was a play that electrified the stadium and made the press box resonate with "oohs" from the most hardened of observers. Elway immediately jumped to his feet, as he so often did after shattering hits, signaled first down, and at that moment the direction this game would take was apparent to all. "We just had to have that first down," he says.

Davis scored two plays later to make it 24-17, but the Packers came back to tie it one last time.

The Denver defense turned back the Packers on their next two possessions, and the Broncos took over at the Green Bay 49-yard line for yet another fourth-quarter drive by Elway, none bigger than this one.

"Those big guys up front really did a great job," Elway explains. "They controlled the line of scrimmage and out-physicalled Green Bay, which is pretty good for the lightest line in the NFL. I sort of sensed in the second half that they (the Packers' linemen) were getting tired. Physically, our line really took it to them."

In five plays for 49 yards—one pass by Elway to fullback Howard Griffith for 23 and the rest runs by Davis—Denver took the lead, 31-24. One minute, 45 seconds remained, and an entire time zone held its breath.

Including Elway. "I was worried about it because we had first-and-goal on the one. I asked when we got to the sideline, 'Do you want to use some time or make them use a timeout?' If we would have known that we were going to get in there that easily, we probably would have wasted a little bit more time. We would have taken a knee or sneak or something. There wasn't anybody around him. Terrell just walked in. It looked like they let us score right away, so they could get the ball back. But it turned out fine.

"It wasn't over until our 'D' stopped them on that final drive. I was just hoping and praying that they would. They had been playing great all day. Favre was one of the best quarterbacks in the league, but they made the plays against him. But when he gets the ball one more time, you're never positive it's over. You're always a little bit worried, especially when they have a guy on the field like Brett. We were all right on the edge of our emotions in those final moments.

"When that last ball hit the ground, it was unbelievable. It was far more than you could ever imagine. The reality was greater than anything I imagined about how great it would be. When (linebacker) John Mobley knocked down Brett's last pass on fourth down, I just went crazy. Do I think of it often? Every day."

Davis had run for 157 of the Broncos' 179 total yards on the ground, and the Broncos scored four times on the ground behind their superb offensive line. Each of the scores was from one yard out, three by Davis and one by Elway himself.

Denver became the first AFC team in 14 years to claim the Vince Lombardi trophy behind a powerful running game and a solid defensive performance.

From all the hype leading up to the game, to the moment when Broncos owner Pat Bowlen hoisted the trophy on the field stage and uttered the phrase, "This one's for John," it was all about finally winning one, taking it all the way for the franchise, the city, and most of all the quarterback.

Elway spilled his feelings, "When I stood there and saw the scoreboard, and all the language on the scoreboard and on the side of the stadium, 'World Champion Denver Broncos,' I just looked at that, and looked at it, and said, 'Man, I can't believe this.'

"You do get tired of being the guy who is perceived as not having won the big game. All those questions I had been answering for all those years, they were finally answered for good."

In addition to snapping the 13-year AFC losing streak, Elway became the first member of the fabled quarterback class of 1983 to win a Super Bowl (that group had been a collective 0-9 until Elway's victory). "Like I said, 'fair' has nothing to do with it. Sometimes things just happen a certain way. Dan Marino and Jim Kelly were great quarterbacks, too, so it was nice to be able to represent the Class of '83 as well.

"That was the ultimate win, without any doubt. There were a lot of things that went along with losing three Super Bowls, and playing for 14 years being labeled as a guy who had never been on a winning Super Bowl team. To finally come out and show them, it's unbelievable."

As he soaked in the moment, Elway took stock. "As I have said so many times, my dad was my hero and my best friend. For us to finally be on the same team and to be able to accomplish that together is something very difficult to put into words. He was my lifelong mentor and the reason why I was able to stand on that podium holding the Vince Lombardi Trophy. He was the best, and I'm just so glad he was always there."

When the Broncos returned to Denver, nearly 700,000 people came out to see the team in a victory parade. "Riding in that parade and just looking at people's faces, experiencing the joy that they felt, made it so much more special. The Broncos have been here for a long, long time and there is a special kinship between the players and the community.

"We were not the only world champions. The people of Denver were world champs too."

AFTER THE CHEERING STOPPED

Immediately upon Elway's retirement, the Broncos Ring of Fame committee waived the five-year waiting period for Denver's highest honor, which in this case was accompanied by the rare retirement of the uniform number.

That was topped off by first-ballot induction into the Pro Football Hall of Fame. "All those honors are humbling, amazing to consider. But everything I accomplished is with the assistance of a lot of other people, and in my case my parents set the stage for my success by how they brought me up."

A highly respected businessman who first jumped into the world of commerce by opening a car dealership early in his career, Elway eventually would have a financial interest in as many as 18 dealerships, and John Elway Auto Nation became a huge part of the Denver landscape for a decade before he moved on to other ventures.

He remains a highly sought-after commercial spokesman, but tries to limit the things to which he says yes. "I prefer to be very selective in that area. I really have to believe in a product before I speak on its behalf. I have numerous other interests, but only so much time."

First and foremost are his four children, and then his charity concerns. "With kids ranging from college to middle school, and all the sports and other extracurricular activities of their lives, retirement from playing gives me a great chance to follow them. But the schedule can really get crazy."

He continues to head a foundation that has funded efforts to prevent child abuse and has given hundreds of college scholarships to students in need.

"When I thought of the great and loving family that nurtured me when I was growing up, and of my own four kids, who really stand alone as the apple of my eye, I knew that was where I wanted to focus my charitable involvement." The Elway Foundation has been a staple of the Denver community for two decades.

But a football guy returns to football and, in time, Elway became owner of the Colorado Crush in the Arena Football League, an expansion team that enjoyed immediate success and won the AFL championship in 2005, giving their boss one more ring, this time as an owner.

"Life is a journey," Elway says. "I just want to keep driving forward, providing guidance to my kids and a positive influence to those I meet along the way.

"It's always the same play, really, for all of us. First down, lifetime to go."

John Elway took the most dramatic step of his post-player career when he assumed his new role as Executive Vice President of Football Operations for the Broncos in 2011. He is in command of all football operations for the Broncos and wasted no time putting his own dramatic stamp on the franchise.

Elway hired the very popular John Fox as the team's new head coach and presided over a club that improved to 8-8 and won a playoff game in his first year heading up the team.

His most recent move was widely acclaimed as the greatest free agent acquisition in NFL history with the signing of future Hall of Famer Peyton Manning. But making a dramatic move is nothing new for the greatest Bronco ever—he has just moved his game from the field to the front office.

The return of Elway to the Broncos is a perfect fit for the team, the city and for John himself as an affirmation of the team's goal of returning to the championship level.

Chapter 21

ROD SMITH

BEFORE THE BRONCOS

Long before Rod Smith became the most prolific undrafted wide receiver in the history of the National Football League, he grew up as poor as poor can be in Texarkana, Arkansas, the middle child of five in a family that had it tough.

"My mom, Lydia Smith, raised me and did everything she could for us as a family. Single mom, five kids, it was very hard for her. Everything she could possibly do to make ends meet, she did, because she raised us as good as she could," he remembers.

He started playing football early, at four or five, just playing in the neighborhood, in the streets, anywhere the local kids could gather.

"I never knew I was better than other kids," Smith said. "All the kids around me were better than me. That's one thing about being down in the ghetto, so to speak. We called them "ghetto superstars." And there literally are, in the ghetto, superstars. The majority of the guys I grew up with were always better than me. So in order to compete, you had to step your game up every single day. There wasn't a day that went by that—in our neighborhood you are going to get challenged all the time, and you are usually challenged by, of course, someone who is better than you all the time. After a while you get tired of losing so you get better."

Recalling the lessons from childhood, Rod Smith says he "never really learned how good I could be, but I kept the same mentality the whole time by always competing against them because I was not as good as them. Since I was competing against them—and of course some of them quit school; some of them went to jail; some of them died—you start climbing the ladder and everybody now is challenging you. I still to this day have friends who when we grew up, they still to this day are better athletes than me and they wonder, 'Well how did you get out and we didn't?' I said, 'It's a thing called discipline. You didn't want to listen to the coach. You thought you had all the answers because in our neighborhood you were a Ghetto Superstar. If I told you how great you were you believed it.' Me? Nobody was telling me how great I was. I always had to work, so I kept working."

No athlete ever mastered discipline or made it work for him any better than Smith.

A high school quarterback whose favorite sport was baseball, he reflects back on his youthful pursuits, "Football just happened. I was not a football player; I loved baseball—I was a baseball player. I always told my sister I was going to make $ 2.5 million playing pro baseball and I was going to give her a million bucks. That's what I used to tell my sister all the time when I was little."

"Wherever they had a spot in baseball, I played. It didn't matter. I played all of them." He pitched and played third base, and in the state championship game "I played shortstop and had the worst game of my life—we lost and I played badly. But eventually, I went all the way to the Super Bowl, so I justified it that way."

In addition to demonstrating discipline at an early age, we see the great competitive edge that marked him from so many other players as a pro.

He knew in high school that he wanted to go to college.

"Absolutely," Smith said. "My sixth grade teacher—I call her my mom, because she's like one of my moms; I've got three moms; I've got two white moms and a black mom—it was Miss Harrison, Donna

Rod Smith was selected for the Denver Broncos Ring of Fame in 2012.
© *Denver Broncos Team Photography*

Harrison, who actually showed me that there was a life outside of the projects. When I walked into her home it really changed my life about college. She's the one who instilled to me I had to go to college. Back in the sixth grade, I was 12 years old and our school was right across the street from the projects. I could look across the street and see our apartment and I could see my mom in the front door. I used to always say, 'I'm going to get my mom out of those projects. I'm going to buy her a house.' I used to say that all the time when I was 12. Miss Harrison always said, 'Well you know you have to go to college.'"

Miss Harrison challenged him, and those who knew him as a pro would attest, you cannot challenge Rod Smith without him responding. "She challenged me that I had to go to go to college. Right then I knew at 12 that I was going to go to college. I didn't know how—I didn't really care—I knew the medium of sports was going to be the way to get me into college. I know my focus in the sixth grade was to get a sports scholarship of some kind. That's why I played every sport—to get a scholarship to go college so I could get out of the projects and go do something better with my life."

ROD SMITH AT A GLANCE

POSITION: Wide Receiver
COLLEGE: Missouri Southern University
PLAYING HEIGHT, WEIGHT: 6-0, 205
YEARS PLAYED FOR BRONCOS: 1994-2007
UNIFORM NUMBER: 80
NOTABLE: Rod Smith was signed by the Broncos as a college free
  agent in 1994 and ended his career as the franchise's all-time
  leader in receptions (849), receiving yards (11,389) and receiv-
  ing touchdowns (68). Smith, who was named to three Pro Bowls
  (2000-01, '05) and was a member of the Denver's back-to-back
  Super Bowl championship teams following the 1997 and '98 seasons, was elected to the Denver Broncos Ring of Fame in 2012.
THE GAME: Super Bowl XXXII, Denver vs. Green Bay, January 25,
1998, San Diego, California

When it came to college there were some smaller schools around Texarkana that gave him a few offers, but Smith played quarterback throughout high school and was not keen on changing positions, as there still were not a lot of black quarterbacks in college at that time, but nobody was going to tell Rod Smith he could not be one. "So I said, 'You know what? If they're not going to let me play quarterback…' I'm going to be a great black quarterback, that was the thing. I'm not playing corner. So I refused to go to those schools." Then Missouri Southern came along and its coach said, 'If you want to play quarterback we will throw the ball a lot.'" And Missouri Southern it was.

He hit the classrooms just as hard as the football fields at Missouri Southern, where he played quarterback and earned not one, or two, but three degrees.

"I was in school my sophomore year and I smashed the arch in my foot. I missed the whole year so they redshirted me. I knew I was going to be at school for five years and my thing is: I don't take classes just to get by. The fall of my last football season my college days were over but I took classes to get me more degrees. When I was sitting with my advisor he had said, 'You know, if you take this class you get two degrees.' I said. 'What does it take to get three?' He looked at me like,

'What? Nobody has ever graduated with three degrees.' I said, 'Good, that's why I want to do it.' That year I was named Outstanding Male Graduate of our entire class, I graduated with three degrees and I was All-American in football. The football stuff came with it but I wanted to prove that I was a true student-athlete."

THE SETTING

Rod Smith always wanted to prove something, and that drive was going to benefit the Denver Broncos in a big way.

So he graduated with degrees in economics, marketing, and business administration, and like a lot of football players, sat back and waited for the NFL draft.

But some things don't work out, and when they don't the resolve is only deepened for individuals like Smith.

The NFL draft came and went, and Smith was not among the more than 200 players selected.

He does not hide his feelings or mince words, ever.

"I hate the draft," Smith steams. "I hate the draft to this day and I still don't watch it. I'm still bitter. I'm not going to lie. I'm still bitter about the draft and probably going to be bitter the rest of my life. I've lived my life with a chip on my shoulder. I watched the draft my whole life. Being in college and doing all the things I did on the football field, I just knew someone was going to give me the chance—you know, sixth round, seventh round. I just wanted to see my name come up on the ticker. You want to hear your name and get one of those big jerseys. The whole thing was a dream of mine and it didn't happen, and it hurt. I still remember lying on the couch for the first day of the draft and not being chosen. The second day, the Kansas City Chiefs called and they said, 'We would like to get you in the third round but you're not fast enough. It hurt and I sat there and waited. I talked to my agent when it was late in the seventh round and he said, 'The Broncos would like to have you as a free agent."

Smith did not even know what it meant to be a free agent. His agent explained that there were no guarantees attached to the Broncos offer, just a chance to make a team starting at the lowest rung of the ladder. This was familiar territory for Smith. He recalls, "I was like, 'Well, it is what it is.' So I talked to head coach Wade Phillips I had never been out of Arkansas, Missouri or Texas—those were the only states I had ever been in. I scoped it out. I looked up Colorado, I looked up Denver. I knew about John Elway, of course, but I just thought, 'I have to get my foot in the door and go to work.'

Smith began his NFL career by playing his way onto the Broncos' practice squad, a nebulous existence subject to change or elimination on any given day. A bad couple of practices and he could be gone. Smith made sure he never had those bad couple of practices. He channeled his past to create a new future.

"It was awesome because I was back in the projects. Being on the practice squad—do you know what it was? It was another ghetto superstar experience and I had to go and prove myself again. That's exactly what it was. It was an exact replica of my growing up. My growing up actually prepared me for being on the practice squad because I watched all the other guys getting the kudos, they get to go on the trips. All I got to do was bring the chicken to the plane and watch them go play and watch the game on TV just like a regular fan. It ticked me off every single day," he remembers. "I never wanted to show that part but it ate at me every day."

At the same time, Smith knew he didn't have NFL receiver skills because he never played the position in college. He had always played quarterback his whole life. "When I played receiver at Missouri Southern I never had a coach. I was just athletic enough to run around, get open and they would throw me the ball and I would make plays," he notes.

In Denver he went about learning the craft. He had to learn how to run routes, a lot of time with his coach yelling at him. A wide receiver on the practice squad has to go against the best cornerbacks every day in practice, so he has to improve against the most extreme odds of success at all times.

Smith created his own game within a game, recalling, "I knew that I could compare my skills to them. Those were the best defensive players we had and I was going against them every single day. I made a game out of it. I said, 'You know what? I'm going to keep my stats during practice because I don't get to go to the game.' So Smith was measuring himself with practice, and his practice stats were like a starting player's game stats.

He remembers having a conversation with cornerback Ray Crockett that he credits with "totally changing my life and my friendship and my relationship with Ray. He would always jam me up because I never had a coach who could tell me how to get off the line or any of that. I asked Ray, I said, 'Man, listen. I watch you kick everybody's butt, mine included, at the line of scrimmage. What am I doing wrong?' He told me, 'Don't raise your arms up. You keep your arms down. You're a big guy, stay low and use your shoulders.' He stayed out to talk to me one time. At first I didn't like Ray because he was cocky. He was rich, he was cocky, and I didn't like him but I had to ask him because I was getting my butt kicked, and I was going to get fired. And I was afraid to get fired. And you know what? He was the nicest guy. He helped me out and every day he would tell me, 'That was better, you did better, it was harder for me to get you today.' Eventually, he couldn't get me at the line anymore."

And Smith knew that if Crockett could not hold him back, neither could anyone else. "He was one of our better corners and I was like, 'If he can't get me then none of you guys are going to be able to get me.' I knew I was going to get the best players and I knew I was going to make plays on those players because I was back in the hood again. I was back in the ghetto playing against some ghetto superstars where you had to outdo them to get their respect. I still remember practice one time, they were running this play in the red zone and I was going against [cornerback] Lionel Washington. We ran it, I caught a touchdown and they said, 'Run it again.' We ran the same play again and I caught it again. They said [to Washington], 'You knew what we were running. Stop him from catching the damn ball.' We did it again and I caught it again. I refused to let him get that ball. Even though they knew what I was doing I refused to let him get that ball. I said, 'I'm going to earn my stripes somehow someway.' Three times straight I caught that ball. I honestly believed I could have caught the ball 10 straight times out of 10 because I was just that focused."

But Smith was still just a practice squad guy, and sometimes making a veteran look bad is not well received by teammates or some coaches.

"I kind of had to play my role. It wasn't anything against Lionel, it was just something I had to do for me."

But finally, a future member of the Pro Football Hall of Fame summed it up in a conversation with head coach Mike Shanahan. Tight end Shannon Sharpe was sitting on a cooler watching Smith make his catches against the fine Broncos corners, and Sharpe said loud enough for all to hear, "Well hell, if they can't cover him in practice then put him in a game. Hell, Coach, they can't cover him in practice. You have to put him in a game. And see what he can do."

Not only did that give Smith more reps in the game but it helped forge a lifelong relationship with Sharpe. "Sharpe kind of played into my practice game with me. It really helped me and motivated me when I would tell him my stats. I was like, 'Sharpe I'm killing these boys. I've got two touchdowns, 145 yards and eight catches.' And then one day he told them what I said…to me it was my game day. That's all I had."

This was about to change.

After spending 1994 on the practice squad and making the active roster the following year, Smith burst into the starting lineup in 1997 with 70 receptions and 12 touchdowns. This was a pattern of success that a disciplined man could make a habit of, and so he did.

The undrafted wide receiver had nine straight years in which his lowest reception total was 70, reaching the 100-catch mark in both 2000 and 2001. He had eight 1,000-yard seasons, including six straight from 1997-2002, and his leadership led his teammates to repeatedly vote the unheralded but driven man from Texarkana as a team captain.

"I had a bunch of different motivations. The internal stuff and the external, which was the environment I grew up in. It was tough and it prepared me for what was going to be even tougher. I tell people still to this day, 'Getting to the NFL is hard as hell; staying in it is even worse.' There are so many people that want that one spot. So you have to be fortunate and you have to take advantage of your opportunities. You can't dwell on what's going on; you have to focus on the now and you have to drive and you have to show them that you're worthy of coming back the next day."

When it was all over and he had played 12 full years for the Broncos, he had more stats than any undrafted wide receiver in NFL history. Smith's career stats stand at 849 receptions, 11,389 yards and 68 touchdowns—all career highs among all NFL undrafted wide receivers, all time.

But the game in which he did not even make a single catch was the one he names as the most significant of that illustrious career.

THE GAME OF MY LIFE

How could the game of his life be one in which the final stats show him as shut out in receptions? Especially as an NFL wide receiver, a position seemingly all about stardom and statistics.

For Rod Smith, it has always been about team, and all about team success.

For Smith and the Broncos, the stars all came together when they defeated the Green Bay Packers to win Super Bowl XXXII. That was the culmination point for a franchise and a star wide receiver that had both started off life deep on the wrong side of the tracks.

"It would be the Super Bowl win over the Packers, when the only time I caught the ball was a punt return and they threw a flag on me for fair-catching the punt. That would be the game of my life. It was a combination of everything: growing up in the projects and trying to make it, playing quarterback and getting moved to receiver, smashing the arch in my foot and getting three degrees because of that, not getting drafted, being on the practice squad and being named a starter in something I had played in the field in the projects. That was the greatest game of my life. The stats didn't matter because the team mattered."

He vividly recalls some key blocks that he and fellow wide receiver Ed McCaffrey had for Super Bowl MVP Terrell Davis. "Just blocking for other guys who caught the ball—just laying it all on the line for the guys next to you, that was it," he emphasized.

Smith ties that game on the world's biggest stage back to his humble beginnings. "We had this game we used to play in my neighborhood called the Creek Bowl because there was a creek right next door. The creek was the sideline. If you got knocked in the creek you were out of bounds and you were going to come up with no skin either. I grew up playing in the Creek Bowl, so I went from the Creek Bowl to the Super

Bowl. I really felt that every guy I ever played against and with in my neighborhood was on the football field with me that day and it was us against everybody else. That's why that was the best game of my life."

That discipline and drive to succeed all came together and was rewarded for all to see. He played a whole career to earn respect and show that he belonged.

The Broncos had entered that game as 14-point underdogs to the Packers, and Smith still seethes at the memory.

"Honestly, I was ticked off because people disrespected the heart of our team. I remember us in the locker room in a meeting and you could just see the focus. When the game was over we were actually mad that we didn't beat them by more because we knew that we were going to beat them by 20-something points. That was our whole focus, to prove a point that all these guys who wear wingtips don't know jack about football because they can't measure heart. We knew we had dominated the football season. You just look at the stats—we dominated the season."

Smith talks about staying up the night before the big game, just watching the various network pundits make their picks, and he was getting steamed. "I still remember Cris Collinsworth saying we were going to get beat. I remember all those guys. It was those numbers that they all said. I was so ticked off, I just got madder and madder. I remember when the game was over and Cris Collinsworth was interviewing me and I said, 'Chris, I can't believe it, you rolled with us all year and you're going to say something stupid. You really disappointed me.' Honestly, it was probably the worst interview ever for him but I was just so angry because I felt disrespected. The guys that I worked with worked so hard as a group. I don't feel bad for what I said because I was in the moment but just the fact that somebody doubted us that bad. We were 14-point underdogs in the Super Bowl. You don't get there by luck."

The Packers drove down the field for the game's first touchdown, and Smith, who always sat on the end of the bench next to Sharpe when the Broncos were on defense, recalls, "The crowd erupted. They scored seven and I saw no one's head drop on our team. No one. Sharpe walked over to me and I got up off the bench. I'm ready to roll and he said, 'They have seven. All we need is eight.' I said, 'Let's go get it.' We went out there and played the best football game ever as a team."

Indeed, one could argue that the entire Denver Broncos franchise, from owner to every single fan, watched and had a part in the team's greatest game that night in San Diego.

The Broncos charged back to tie the score on a run by Davis and never looked back. Elway ran for a TD in the second period, kicker Jason Elam kicked a field goal and Denver took a 17-14 lead into the intermission. In the second half the Packers could not keep up with the Broncos running game as Davis scored twice more on one-yard runs, with the Broncos rushing for 179 yards overall in their dominating 31-24 win over the Packers.

Denver ran the ball 39 times to just 22 passes by Elway and controlled time of possession, holding the ball and the game for 32:25 minutes against Green Bay.

And through it all, most of what Rod Smith did was block. He touched the ball just once, that on a punt return negated by penalty, so the final offensive stats from Super Bowl XXXII show no mention of his name.

But the only numbers that mattered to Smith were the ones on the scoreboard, flashing on the big screen next to the picture of team owner Pat Bowlen hoisting the Vince Lombardi trophy..

"We had a bunch of misfits. I still remember 'Stink' [guard Mark Schlereth] calling us the 'misfits' because nobody wanted a lot of the guys that were on that team. There were a lot of outcasts, so to speak. There weren't a bunch of first-round picks. I think we had two first-round picks that were starters and the rest of us were outcasts from other group, but our staff did an excellent job of putting a bunch of hungry dogs together."

The Broncos knew how to win, collectively and because of individuals like free agent Smith. "It all comes back to discipline," he preaches again and again. "Why my friends were better and more athletic than me and what we called ghetto superstars and why they never made it—it was discipline. There is something about following the rules that some people don't get."

He has always carried his core values over to all aspects of his life, not just his world on the football field. "Some people think they get to call all of the shots. I always reinforce to my kids [Smith has a daughter and two sons], 'You don't call the shots. I do.' It's not that I'm trying to call the shots to make you a lesser person, it's because you have to have that discipline when I'm not there, or you're never going to make it in this world. You have to be able to operate on certain principles that can never be deviated from regardless of the situation or circumstances."

AFTER THE CHEERING STOPPED

Retired from football and pursuing new successes in the business world, Smith is kept busy taking a hands-on approach to his investments, but he has never forgotten those who helped him become a Broncos legend and a certain future Ring of Famer for the team.

Always reflective, he pauses to credit others. "To this day, I always give Wade Phillips credit for just giving me the opportunity. Every time I see him, even if he is coaching another team and I see him on the field before the game, I approach him and say, 'Wade, if you didn't give me the chance I wouldn't have had a chance.' And he says, 'You did it.' And it went from him to Mike Shanahan, who put those consecutive championship teams together, and to the late Mike Heimerdinger."

Heimerdinger, who passed away due to illness in 2011, was Smith's receiver coach for those back-to-back title winners in Denver. Smith failed to hold back tears when he said, "I'm always going to have the utmost respect for Mike Heimerdinger. It hurts me now that he's not here because my life won't be the same without Mike Heimerdinger taking time with me and just giving me a chance. I'm always going to have the utmost respect for Coach Shanahan as well because he believed in me and he got rid of guys for me and I never wanted to let him down."

One thing that every Bronco fan could attest to—Rod Smith never let anybody down.

He still lives in the Denver area and focuses on investments, and he still does it his way.

"Right now I'm in the coffee business. I'm with a network marketing company and I love saying that because people sometimes hate that word 'marketing' because they equate it with some plan that didn't work. But ours is a healthier coffee company and we are doing amazing right now."

Smith says his firm is doing very well with high volume sales, "all from where I'm sitting right now at my desk. My thing is I love to teach. Financially, I've watched people make more money than they've ever made in their life, and on a part-time basis. I get to coach that."

"I get to coach people in the game of their life," he says. "That's what I get my kicks out of now. I get to celebrate their success. People say, 'Rod, you're doing well because you played for the Broncos.' I say, 'No, I'm doing well because I have certain successful habits and I take those habits on every avenue that I go.'"

"By the way, I want the Broncos to put my coffee in their stadium. Put that in the book. For one thing, it's great coffee for people; it makes them feel better. We also serve a lot of causes because it's bigger than just me."

In retirement, Smith's life is just like it was before, always aggressively looking to the future, never to the past which set the stage.